Planes & Pilots

SUPERMARINE SPITFIRE
Mark VI - Mark VII - Mark VIII - Mark IX & Mark XVI
Volume II

Phil LISTEMANN

Colour profiles by Bill Dady
Translated from the French by Lawrence Brown

HISTOIRE & COLLECTIONS

Supermarine SPITFIRE Mk.VI to IX and Mk.XVI

By 1941, the Spitfire's career was well under way and the RAF had at its disposal a high performance aircraft with the Mk.V, a version that corresponded well to its requirements at that time. Supermarine and the RAF were already preparing a successor to the Mk.V and new versions were on the drawing board as, during wartime, the race to invent new armaments was constant and a plane had to be continually upgraded to avoid becoming obsolete and, if possible, had to always perform better than its adversaries.

In 1941 therefore, the successor to the Mk.V was already being designed, not counting certain versions that answered specific RAF requirements. However, the Spitfire also had to deal with emergency situations that could have put an end to its brilliant career.

Top.
Three-quarter view of the Spitfire Mk.VI, a Spitfire version designed for high altitude intercepting. Seen from this angle, once can make out the differences that characterise this version, a four-blade propeller, pointed wingtips and, under the exhaust vents, part of the pressurisation system that was not always reliable or liked by the pilots and ground crew.
However, the results of the Mk.VI as a fighter were neither better nor worse than most of he units equipped with the Spitfire Mk.V at that time. No 124 Sqn., to which the plane seen here belongs to, obtained good results against the Luftwaffe.

The Spitfire Mk.VI

The Spitfire MK. VI was not a version designed to replace the Mk.V in frontline units, but rather one that was designed to meet the requirements of the RAF which, in 1941, was looking for a fighter capable

Previous page at the bottom and top.
The Spitfire Mk.VII, which was also designed for high-altitude interception, was a new and much better aircraft than the Spitfire Mk.VI, even if its exterior resemblance is striking. 140 of these planes were built and it had a discreet career due to its somewhat late arrival within units at a time when the Luftwaffe rarely flew over the British Isles. Most were delivered with a camouflage scheme reserved for reconnaissance Spitfires, but when, in 1944, they were progressively used at lower altitudes, they began to be painted in the Day Fighter Scheme, as seen with this plane of No 131 Sqn. seen here at the end summer 1944, a few weeks before its withdrawal.

Top.
F. VII prototype (serial AB 450) was tested at the AAEE of Boscombe Down from September 1942.

Bottom.
Mk VI serial X4942 was in fact a modified Mark I which first flight occurred on 26 June 1942.

of flying at a much higher altitude than the Mk.V in order to intercept German reconnaissance aircraft flying at very high altitude and which remained out of the reach of conventional Spitfires. Consequently, Supermarine developed the Mk.VI which was in fact a Mk.V equipped with a pressurised cockpit and an engine suited for high altitude flying, the 1,415 HP Merlin 47 powering a four-blade propellor, something that was a first for the Spitfire.

In order to fly at high altitude where the air was more rarefied, and thus retain sufficient lift, the wingtips were lengthened, giving the aircraft a distinctive outline. Two prototypes flew in 1941 and the subsequent trials were deemed as success.

The requirements of such an aircraft were by definition limited, a small production run of 100 planes was ordered by the RAF but, in fact only 97 aircraft were effectively signed over to the RAF; all in 1942. These aircraft were delivered in sporadic batches and the Mk.VI were

in fact Mk.V airframes taken off the assembly lines and then transformed.

Only two frontline units would use the Mk.VI, Nos 124 and 616 Squadron, the Mk.VI remained operational between June 1942 and September 1943, the period in which this version claimed the destruction of twenty German planes and the flying of approximately 5,000 sorties.

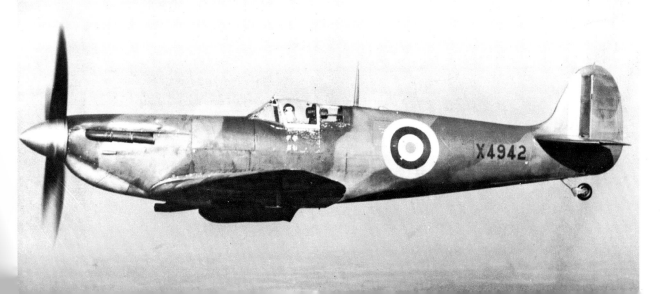

Seen in flight, Spitfires of No 349 Sqn. (Belgian), armed with bombs, flying towards their objective in late summer 1944. This squadron was then the only Belgian unit (among two) to use the Mk.IX, since squadron No 350 had switched to the Mk.XIV. No 349 Sqn. finished the war with the Mk.XVI. (André Bar)

Contrary to what is commonly believed, it turns out that this version was neither better nor worse than the Mk.V from an operational point of view. Indeed, the Mk.VI is often considered as being the least powerful of all the Spitfires, but it is above all the bad luck of No 616 Sqn (seven kills for twenty losses) which is at the origin of this commonly held belief, which appears unjustified if we take into account the tally of No 124 Sqn (thirteen kills for five losses), which is better than some units equipped with the Spitfire Mk.V, or even the Mk. IX!

On the other hand, the pilots and ground crews who used the Mk.VI, did not always like its sometimes tricky pressurisation system, and it was above all this reason that led the RAF to withdraw the Mk.VI after little more than a year of operational service. The surviving Mk.VI Spitfires would often be used to complete units sent for a rest period far from the frontline, something which allowed many pilots to familiarise themselves with high altitude flying and the equipment associated with such flights. However, the Mk.VI became of great use, from 1943 onwards, within weather reconnaissance units where its high altitude

capabilities were extremely appreciated. Finally, the Mk.VI would be taken out of service before the end of hostilities in Europe.

Some planes were also sent to the Middle-East in 1942 in order to intercept the Luftwaffe Junkers Ju 86P which were flying over Egypt, however this was short-lived due to the pressurisation system that turned out to be ill-suited for the local weather conditions.

The Spitfire Mk.VII

The Spitfire Mk.VII, even though it remained a fighter made for high altitude interception, was not exactly an improved Mk.VI, despite looking very much the same from the outside. Its airframe concealed important modifications compared to the Mk.VI whilst at the same time remaining a pressurised fighter. The Mk.VII had been strengthened and modified in order to carry more fuel, and the ailerons and wings were also greatly modified (apart from the first planes built), whilst the entire production run saw the installation of a retractable tail wheel that

The Mk.VIII should have been the main Spitfire version by taking over from the Mk.V in fighter units from 1942 onwards. However, the unexpected arrival of the Fw 190 changed things and the Spitfire Mk.IX carried out this role splendidly to the detriment of the Mk.VIII. The plane seen here is one of the last Mk.VIII to be built, MT635, which would be sent to Australia, flying under the serial number of A58-543.

had already been tested out on the Spitfire Mk.III.

As for its engine, several versions of the Merlin were installed on the Spitfire Mk.VII: first the 61, then the 64, both of which were optimised for high altitude flying.

The first Mk.VII left the production lines in August 1942 and, up to May 1944, another 139 were delivered to the RAF. As with the Mk.VI, the Mk.VII was not the subject of a separate order and all were taken from the assembly lines of the Spitfire Mk.V already officially ordered.

From an operational point of view, the Mk.VII progressively replaced the Mk.VI within Nos 124 and 616 Squadrons, to which was added in 1944, No 131 Squadron where, globally, it was better liked by the pilots and ground crews. These three units were those which used the Mk.VII intensively in combat. The Mk.VII would have a low-key career, only flying approximately 6,500 sorties and claiming twenty kills, that is to say hardly more than the Mk.VI. It was withdrawn from operational service during the course of autumn 1944 (even though No 154 Sqn was briefly equipped with them at the beginning of 1945). However, like the Mk.VI, it would also render great service to the weather reconnaissance units up to the end of the war. Some aircraft continued flying after the war and the last of them were struck off charge in 1947.

Given the low number built, the Mk.VII finally had a low-key career, but it carried out its role as a high altitude interceptor perfectly before the Luftwaffe stopped entering British airspace, thus obliging the RAF to attribute a more offensive role to its bomber escorts, starting in the spring of 1944.

The Spitfire Mk.VIII

The Spitfire Mk.VIII was in fact a non-pressurised version of the Mk.VII designed for low altitude combat. At the outset, it was the designated successor to the Mk.V, the replacement of which was planned from 1943 onwards. However, due to a slower than planned for development, the first aircraft did not leave the assembly lines until November 1942. At this time, the Mk.IX had recently entered into service within Fighter Command and appeared to have a bright future ahead of it. With the impending arrival of the first Griffon-engined Spitfires, the RAF decided to retain the Mk.VIII for overseas theatres of operations,

that is to say, the Mediterranean, Far-East and the Pacific where the replacement of the Spitfire Mk.V had become a necessity.

The arrival of the Mk.IX sealed forever the fate of this version, often considered as being the most fully developed, but whose career was overshadowed by that of the Mk.IX. The official number of Mk.VIII built is 1,658, 75% being delivered with a Merlin 66 providing maximum power at low altitude, with the others being delivered with either the F.VIII configuration (273 with the Merlin 63) or HF.VIII (160 with the Merlin 70). The last Mk.VIII were taken on charge in December 1944.

It was in the Mediterranean that the Mk.VIII first entered into service at the end of spring 1943, however it was in the Far-East that it was most used as just under half of those made were sent there starting at the end of 1943.

In the Pacific, there were no less than 410 that would come under the control of the RAAF, including almost all of the HF.VIII (159 aircraft). Even though the Mk.VIII remained a high performance aircraft in 1945, the RAF had to rationalise its versions at the end of the war and the Mk.IX and Mk.XVI were therefore chosen over the Mk.VIII which was then withdrawn from service in the month following the end of the war against Japan.

The Mk.VIII pilots only claimed approximately 150 kills (confirmed or probable), two-thirds of which were in the Mediterranean, a figure which appears little but which can be mostly explained by the fact that this version was used in regions where the air opposition was weak, or even inexistent. Also, although this excellent fighter was used as a priority for this mission, by the end of the war it was only used in a ground support role.

With the 2 TAF, the Spitfire Mk.IX played a dual role, as it was used both as a fighter and fighter-bomber. In the autumn of 1944, when the Griffon-engined Spitfire arrived at the 2 TAF, its role was almost exclusively that of a fighter-bomber, as we can see here on this plane belonging to No 132 Sqn. during its rearming with three bombs. The Spitfire Mk.IX's sole major fault was its incapacity to carry rockets under its wings and the fact that it was armed with small-calibre machine-guns. This last point was corrected as American issue .50 calibre were introduced in the autumn of 1944.

The Spitfire Mk.IX

The Spitfire Mk.IX is probably one of the best known versions of the Spitfire. However, this version should never have existed in this form... Its creation can in fact be attributed to the appearance at the end of 1941 of the Focke Wulf Fw 190A over the Western Front. The RAF pilots were quick to state that the Spitfire Mk.V, the standard RAF fighter at this time in Great Britain, was outclassed in many aspects of flight by the new German fighter. The RAF, therefore, had to quickly find a solution and improve the Spitfire. Working with a sense of urgency, Supermarine installed a Merlin 61, which was undergoing trials at the time, in a Mk.V airframe in order to boost its performance. The Merlin 61 was more powerful than the previous engines and, coupled with a four-blade propellor and other aerodynamic refinements, it gave the Spitfire what

Top.
Mark VIII serial JF299 served as a test-bed and received a tear-drop canopy in September 1943. It was equipped with a Mk.XII tail and had clipped wings. It was put back to Mk.VIII standards in November 1943.

had been missing with the Mk.V in order to take on the 'Würger' (Shrike, the Fw 190's nickname). The results were such that the RAF attributed the Mk.IX denomination to this new version and introduced it as quickly as possible into its units during the course of the summer of 1942. The first Mk.IX were made by modifying the Spitfire Mk.V as it left the assembly lines. Despite a difficult start, the Mk.IX soon showed what it was capable of, to such an extent that by 1944, it had become the standard RAF fighter and had totally taken over from the Mk.V in frontline units. This 'interim' version in fact upset the order, as the Mk.VIII, which was sup-

Spitfire Mk.IX BS289 was one of the first Spitfires of this version to be put into service. Hurriedly designed to counter the arrival of the Fw 190, the Mk.IX turned out to be the plane that the RAF required at that precise time. Very closely resembling the Spitfire Mk.V from which it was derived, it caught a great many German pilots by surprise at the beginning. No-one thought, in 1942, that the Mk.IX would become one of the highest scoring versions of this legendary fighter.

posed to take over from the Mk.V in fighter units, was in some ways sacrificed and relegated to a secondary rôle before finally being sent far from Great Britain and, therefore, the limelight!

The production of the Mk.IX was slowed down by a lack of Rolls Royce Merlin 61 engines, forcing Supermarine to maintain production of the Mk.V up to the end of the summer of 1943. However, from these date onwards, the production of the Mk.IX was well under way and to such an extent that when the last Mk.IX were delivered to the RAF in June 1945, more than 5,600 of this version had left the production lines; with this figure taking into account the conversions carried out on later versions.

Production of the Mk.IX was such that Great Britain ceded more than a thousand of this version to the Soviets as part of the Lend Lease Act, starting at the end of 1943.

The Mk.IX was made during three years and the modifica-

The prototype of the twin-seater Spitfire N32, was in fact a former Mk.VIII (MT818) transformed using Vickers-Armstrong money. Making its maiden flight in 1946, it appeared in public in September of the same year, painted entirely in yellow. Later, only twenty Spitfires would be modified into T.IX, not counting the twin-seaters made by the Soviets, the number of which is not known.

tions made to the basic version were few. Only the armament was upgraded in autumn 1943, the four .303 machine-guns, now totally obsolete, were replaced with American-made .50 calibre machine-guns. A few dozen of this version were also modified during the war in order to carry photographic equipment, thus enabling them to carry out tactical reconnaissance missions, particularly in the Mediterranean.

However, in June 1945, the rate of loss of the planes was high

Line up of Spitfire Mk IXe from the No 111 Squadron; JU°F is in the foreground.

and in fact corresponded to the major role played by the Mk.IX in the war in the air over Europe in 1944-45. When the war came to an end in Europe, the RAF only had 2,200 Mk.IX in its units or stores. If we take from this number the 1,100 aircraft delivered to the Soviets and the few dozen lost by the Americans in the Mediterranean, the RAF had, therefore, lost approximately half of its Mk.IX that it had taken on charge between 1942 and 1945. This rate of loss continued in the following months as dozens of planes damaged by the enemy of just simply worn out from months of intensive use, were simply struck off charge.

After the war, the Mk.IX was deemed obsolete, notably when compared to Spitfire versions equipped with the Griffon engine and, above all to the new kings of the sky, the jet aircraft. The Mk.IX's days were therefore numbered, but as Great Britain needed both money and to assert its influence, it decided to offer the Mk.IX for exportation. This choice was also dictated by the fact that the Mk.XVI, the twin of the Mk.IX with its American-made engine and, therefore, financed by the United States via the Lend Lease Act, was the object of specific terms of use as the engines were officially considered as being the property of the United States government until they were totally paid for, something that did not happen until much later.

Thus, in the first years following the end of the war, approximately 1,200 Mk.IX swapped their RAF roundels for those of other countries to whom they were sold or ceded under more or less advantageous conditions. After 1947, the Mk.IX was less used, unlike the Mk.XVI which would continue to be used. However, in total, during the Second World War, more than a hundred fighter units would be totally or partially equipped with the Spitfire.

It should be noted that this version saw a twin-seater version after the war, known under the denomination of Spitfire T.IX, in reality a transformation of already existing single-seaters and not a newly made aircraft. The Soviets had the same idea and they too transformed a few of their Mk.IX into twin-seaters.

The Spitfire Mk.XVI

The Spitfire Mk.XVI was not, strictly speaking, a specific version, but was in fact a Mk.IX powered by a Merlin 266 made by Packard in the United States. Indeed, the decision to make the Rolls Royce Merlin in the United States was taken in view of producing more Mk.IX, the production of which was insufficient at the time to cover the needs of the RAF. The version chosen was the 1,580 HP Merlin 66 designed for low altitude flying. The first engine arrived in Great Britain at the end of year and was fitted to a Mk.IX, MJ556, which carried out its maiden flight in December 1943. Subsequent trials were satisfactory.

However, due to the use of the metric system and several internal changes, the Merlin 266 was not an exact copy of the Merlin 66, and maintenance of these engines demanded specific tools. In order to find a solution to these logistical problems, the Mk.IX and Mk.XVI could not be used in the same operational unit, it was decided to attribute a specific designation to aircraft with these engines. Therefore, the Spitfires equipped with the Merlin 266 thus became the Mark XVI. It should be noted that this difference only applied to the RAF as Supermarine called both the 'Type 361'.

Full production was reached in the United States during the summer of 1944 and the first engines could start being mounted on production Spitfires the following autumn with both versions, the Mk.IX and Mk.XVI, being produced at the same time on the same assembly line depending on the arrival of Merlin 266 engines from the United States. As they were designed for low altitude flying, most of the Mk.XVI were delivered with clipped wings, whereas they all had a pointed tail fin.

The first were equipped with type 'C' armaments, but the Mk.XVI also arrived on time to be equipped with the 'E' wing

Spitfire JF321 originally ordered as a Mk.VIII, was fitted with de Havilland contra-props and an enlarged fin before being modified as a Mark XIV.

After the war, many high ranking officers attached to headquarters used Spitfires as a personal plane. For this reason, some of these planes had somewhat particular post-war careers. This was the case with SL721, seen here with Air Marshall James M. Robb on board, whose code comprises of his initials ("JMR").

and its .50 calibre machine-guns. It was also this model which introduced the teardrop canopy, from February 1945 onwards. The Mk.XVI massively equipped the Spitfire units of the 2 TAF and Fighter Command used in bombing missions over continental Europe flown from British territory. Deliveries logically stopped in June 1945 with the end of hostilities in Europe. At this time, a little more than 1,050 Mk.XVI had been taken on charge by the RAF and 900 still figured in its inventory. In the weeks which followed, several dozen aircraft, damaged in combat or in accidents, were struck off charge in order to avoid costly repairs which were now of no use and, in any case, the RAF already had surplus aircraft to deal with.

The Mk.XVI's post-war career carried on well beyond the nineteen-fifties. As the Mk.IX had already been chosen at the time as the first export Spitfire, the Mk.XVI, of which many were still in stores, would logically replace the Mk.IX in RAF units based in Great Britain, the number of which had greatly diminished whilst awaiting the bringing into service of jet aircraft. The quantity of Merlin 266 engines, delivered as part of the Lend Lease agreement, was sufficient to keep these few dozen Mk.XVI in service for a few years. The RAF even had, in 1947-48, a surplus of these aircraft of which it did not hesitate to sell off with the permission of the Americans, with approximately 80 Mk.XVI being sent to Greece which was in the throes of a civil war. In all, almost fifty squadrons would fly with the Mk.XVI during and after the war, but only twenty units flew operational sorties (more than 20,000), before 8 May 1945.

Mk XVIE serial SL718 fom the No 612 (County of Aberdeen) Squadron of the RAuxAF photographed at Elmdon during the Cooper Air Race, in July 1949, with its race number.

Mark VI

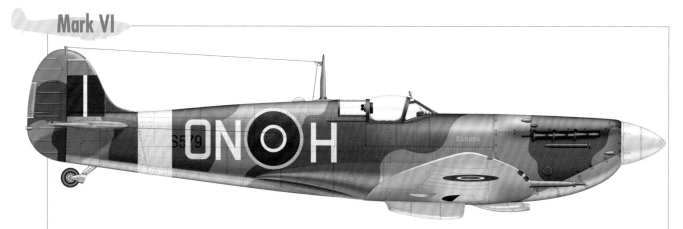

Supermarine Spitfire Mk.VIB BR579, Pilot Officer Michael P. 'Slim' Kilburn, No 124 (Baroda) Squadron. Debden (Great Britain), Summer 1942.
No 124 Squadron was one of the two units that used the Spitfire Mk.VI operationally. In a little over 1,000 sorties, the squadron claimed a dozen victories. 3,5 of them scored by Pilot Officer Kilburn flying BR579, 3,5 represents more than half his tally of kills. He survived the war. It is worth noting the almost faded "Baroda" painted in the front of the cockpit canopy.

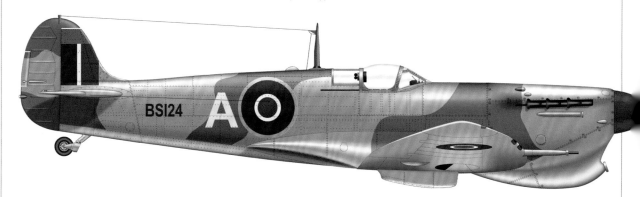

Supermarine Spitfire Mk.VIB/Trop BS124 of the High Altitude Flight from the No 103 Maintenance Unit. Aboukir (Egypt), Autumn 1942.
Half a dozen Mk.VI were sent to Egypt in order to try and intercept the Ju 86R that flew regularly over the region. However, they were rapidly taken out of service as they proved to be unable to gain the altitudes at which the Ju 86 flew, and also because the pressurisation system was unreliable.

Mark VII

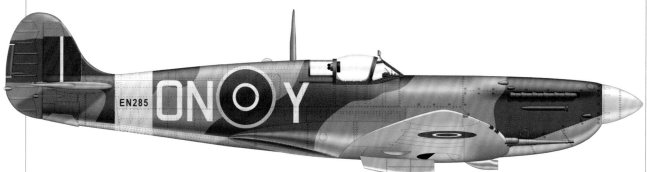

Supermarine Spitfire HF.VII EN285 of No 124 (Baroda) Squadron. North Weald (Great Britain), Spring 1943.
No 124 was the first squadron to be equipped with the Mk.VII. The model was better received than the Mk.VI. A dozen victories were claimed in fifteen months of use. In July 1944, the Mk.VII was replaced with the Spitfire HF.IX which were made for high-altitude flight.

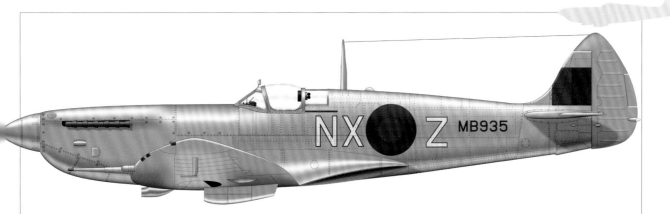

Supermarine Spitfire HF.VII MB935. W/O Douglas F. Philipps (RAAF). No 131 (County of Kent) Squadron. Harrowbear (Great Britain), 23 April 1944.
The MB935 was among the first of the Spitfire Mk. VII to be assigned to No 131 Sqn. in February 1944. This plane was lost with its Australian pilot on 23 April 1944: he was scrambled but crashed at sea in circumstances that remain unknown to this day. The aircraft is painted with the colours reserved to high-altitude planes, apart from its code letters, that have a black edging, something that was an infringement on the regulations seen on a few this unit's planes in the first weeks of use.

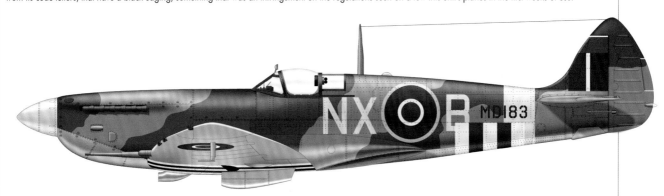

Supermarine Spitfire HF.VII MD183. No 131 (County of Kent) Squadron. Culmhead (Great Britain), July 1944.
MD183 arrived at No 131 Sqn. in mid-June, and was used by this unit until it was declared non-operational in October. It is one of the few Mk.VIIs of the squadron that bore the standard Fighter Command camouflage scheme along with invasion stripes, the sizes of which were modified in July. No 131 Sqn. claimed half a dozen kills with the Mk.VII (including the very last victories for this type) on 7 August 1944.

Supermarine Spitfire HF.VII MD168. No 154 Squadron. Biggin Hill (Great Britain), early 1945.
After having fought in the Mediterranean for many years, No 154 Sqn. was reformed in Great Britain where it was given the Mk.VII left by No 132 Sqn. after their departure for the Far East. MD168, seen here, was one of these planes. From 1 February 1945 onwards, this squadron led escort missions for Bomber Command, but switched to the Mustang Mk.IV in the middle of this month.

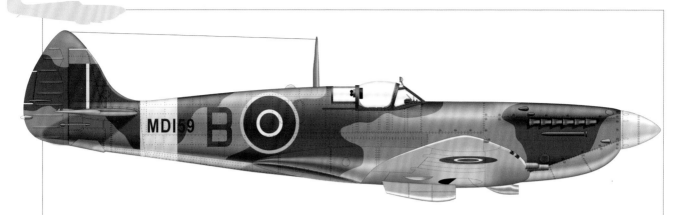

Supermarine Spitfire HF.VII MD159. No 518 Squadron. Aldergrove (Great Britain), autumn 1945.
The versions designed for high-altitude flight were of great aid to the weather reconnaissance units. Consequently, a certain number of Spitfire Mk.VII were used within these squadrons, which were equipped with various types of planes. This is the case with MD159 seen here, which joined No 518 Sqn. in September 1945.

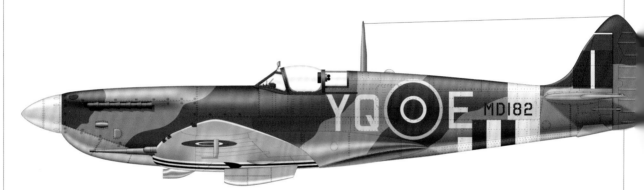

Supermarine Spitfire HF.VII MD182. No 616 (South Yorkshire) Squadron. Culmhead (Great Britain), July 1944.
No 616 Sqn. received the Mk. VII in September 1943, which they kept until August 1944. The squadron was not luckier with the Mk.VII than it had been with the Mk.IV, as it only scored a few victories in one year. No 616 ended up by stopping flying Spitfires and became the first operational RAF squadron equipped with Meteors.

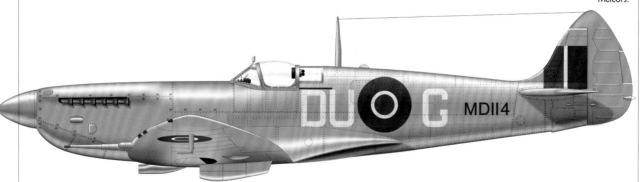

Supermarine Spitfire HF.VII MD114. Station Flight Skaebrae. Skaebrae (Great Britain), February 1944.
Even thought MD114 bore the "DU" code of the Czechoslovakian No 312 Sqn., this plane was actually used by the Station Flight based in Skaebrae, Scotland. In fact, No 312 Sqn. had stayed at this base a few months earlier during a rest period, and, like all units in the same situation, they had taken on charge old Spitfire models in order to leave the new ones for the squadrons on the front line. The Station Flight probably inherited these codes during their stay at Skaebrae. In the RAF, the double use of unit codes in the same theatre of operations was rare, but in this case, consequences were negligible, as No 312 was based much further south. It is worth noting the lack of a yellow border around the fuselage roundel, which was probably made out of a red and blue roundel, which would lead to the conclusion that the lower surface roundels were also added. The presence of yellow leading edges, which were usually absent on high-altitude fighters, might mean that this plane was no longer used as a high-altitude interceptor.

Supermarine Spitfire LF.VIII JG614. No 17 Squadron. Vavuniya (Ceylon), Summer 1944.
In the spring of 1944, No 17 Sqn. was one of the first fighter units based in the Far East to be equipped with the Spitfire Mk.VIII. In November 1944, as it was based in Ceylon, the squadron was sent to the continent under the command of "Ginger" Lacey, the famous Battle of Britain ace. No 17 kept its Mk.VIII planes until June 1945. It is worth noting the lack of "YB" codes, which were normally attributed to this squadron - it seems that the codes were painted on once they were based on the continent. The squadron claimed half a dozen victories against the Japanese with the Mk.VIII in approximately 3,000 sorties.

Supermarine Spitfire LF.VIII MT714. W/O R. L. Oliver (RCAF). No 43 Squadron. Ramatuelle (France), August 1944.
No 43 Sqn., which used the Mk.IX from November 1943 onwards, was equipped with Mk.VIII starting in mid-August for a few weeks in order to provide air cover for the Provence landings, as the Mk.VIII's range and speed were better suited to the squadron's missions. In October, No 43 switched back to its Mk.IX planes and kept them until the end of the war.

Supermarine Spitfire LF.VIII A58-480. No 54 Squadron. Livingstone (Australia), August 1944.
In 1942, No 54 was sent to Australia to fend off a possible Japanese invasion. The squadron first used the Mk.V, before switching to the Mk.VIII in March 1944, which they kept until the end of the war. The squadron only claimed two victories in their 18-month use of the Mk.VIII.

Supermarine Spitfire LF.VIII LV675. F/L Harry « Pat » Pattison (RCAF). No 67 Squadron.Akyab (Burma), Spring 1945.
No 67 Sqn. was among the first Hurricane units to switch to the Spitfire Mk.VIII in February 1944. The Canadians did not deploy any fighter units in the Far East, but they were present in great numbers in that region, such as "Pat" Pattison, who was there from November 1944 to April 1945. Seen here is a plane bearing the rapid reconnaissance markings introduced in late 1944 during the recapture of Burma.

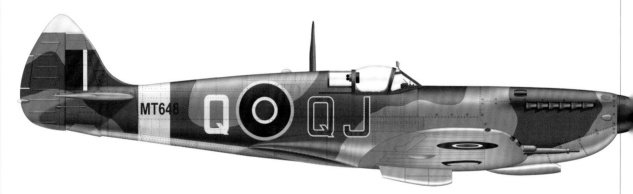

Supermarine Spitfire LF.VIII MT648. Major John E. Gasson (SAAF). No 92 (East India) Squadron. Bellaria (Italy), Spring 1945.
No 92 Sqn. was one of the few fighter units in the Mediterranean to use the Mk.VIII until the end of the war. They were issued with the planes in July 1943. Since October 1944, this unit was led by Major Gasson, from South Africa, one of the rare members of the SAAF to be decorated with the DSO and DFC and Bar. No 92 claimed thirty victories in two years with the Mk. VIII.

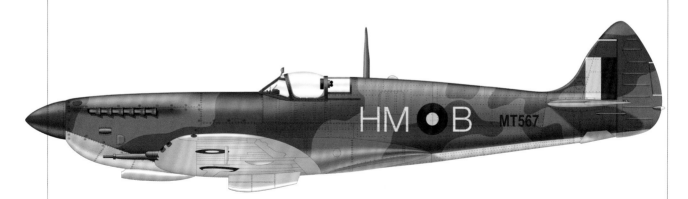

Supermarine Spitfire LF.VIII MT567. No 136 Squadron. Coco Islands, Summer 1945.
In the autumn of 1943, No 136 Sqn. was one of the three fighter units to introduce the Spitfire in the Far East. It was a logical step when they switched from the Mk.V to the Mk.VIII in January 1944, becoming operational with this type a month later. The squadron kept its Mk.VIII Spitfires until November 1945.

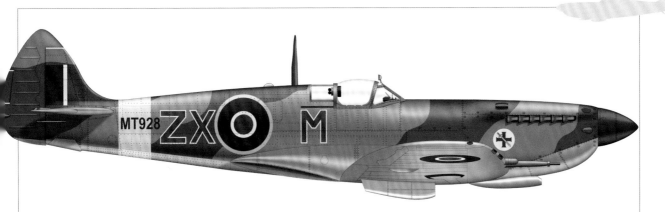

Supermarine Spitfire LF.VIII MT928, No 145 Squadron, Fano (Italy), autumn 1944.
After claiming many victories in North Africa with the Mk.V, No 145 Sqn. received the Mk.VIII in June 1943, which they kept until the end of the war, even though it also used Mk.IX for a few weeks. Approximately 40 kills were achieved with the Mk.VIII, the last of which were claimed in the spring of 1944. The white-bordered red codes were a distinctive sign of this squadron. The Cross of Malta, which comes from the No 145's insignia, was added in late 1944. The camouflage scheme was that of the Fighter Command, which at that time had only been introduced since a few weeks previously.

Supermarine Spitfire LF.VIII MV142, No 152 (Hyderabad) Squadron. Tengah (Singapore), early 1946.
No 152 Sqn. was equipped with Spitfires as early as December 1939. The squadron was sent to the Mediterranean in late 1942 after three years of being based on British soil. At the end of 1943, the squadron arrived in India, where it was issued with the Mk.VIII; this squadron, therefore, was one of the rare units to have used five different versions of Spitfires: the Mk.I, II, V, IX and VIII. Note the serial painted in the tailplane identification stripe.

Supermarine Spitfire LF.VIII JF880. No 417 (RCAF) Squadron (RCAF). Fano (Italy), early 1945.
No 417 Sqn. was the only Canadian fighter unit to be created during the war to fight in the Mediterranean. Another particularity is the fact that the unit fought exclusively with the Mk.VIII, from August 1943 to the end of the war, just like three other fighter squadrons in the sector. The squadron claimed around 30 victories during this period. At its delivery in September 1943, the JF880 was probably supposed to be painted with the "Temperate land Scheme". It was first lent to the USAAF, then returned to the RAF in the spring of 1944. The plane was taken on charge by No 417 in December 1944, where it was repainted with the standard Fighter Command camouflage scheme, but retained its red propellor cone; the leading edges of its wings were not painted yellow either.

Supermarine Spitfire LF.VIII MT687. No 451 (RAAF) Squadron. Gargano (Italy), autumn 1944.
The Australian No 451 Sqn. was originally a tactical reconnaissance unit for the army, but in February 1943, it was converted to a standard fighter unit. It was kept away from combat zones at first, before being sent to the front lines in April 1944. The following August, the squadron was issued with the Mk.VIII that they used along with Mk.IX. In November, No 451 departed for the United Kingdom and left the Mk.VIII to the other units. The Koogagoora seen here is meant to clearly show where the pilot comes from!

Supermarine Spitfire LF.VIII A58-504. F/O Rex W. Watson. No 452 (RAAF) Squadron. Tarakan (Dutch Indies), July 1945.
No 452 Sqn. exchanged its Mk.V for the Mk.VIII in January 1945. The squadron was first tasked with defending Darwin, but was subsequently sent the Dutch Indies in late 1944, where it stayed until the end of the war, and claiming two victories there. A58-504 was flown by F/O Rex Watson, who had already gained recognition in Darwin in 1943, where he had scored a few kills. His favourite insignia was Walt Disney's "Jiminy Cricket", that we can find on a great number of his planes. The lack of a tailplane flag remains unexplained, but infringements of regulations regarding markings in this region were frequent in 1945. In Australia, A58-504 was repainted with the Foliage Green and Sky blue camouflage scheme, the RAAF's specific scheme.

Supermarine Spitfire LF.VIII A58-457. S/L Thomas H. Trimble. No 457 (RAAF) Squadron. Sattler (Australia), July 1944.
Just like No 452, the No 457 Sqn. switched from the Mk.V to the Mk.VIII in 1944. S/L Trimble, who had fought in the desert war, chose A58-457 as his personal plane. Squadron leaders often preferred the letter Z over the letter A (which was normally reserved to them). The Spitfire, which seems to have been repainted with the Australian Earth Brown (a scheme close to the British scheme of Dark Brown, Foliage Green and Sky Blue). No 457 Sqn.'s only victory claimed with the Mk.VIII was on 20 June 1945. It is worth noting the white rapid recognition stripes on the leading edges.

Supermarine Spitfire LF.VIII A58-482. S/L Ernest D. Glaser. No 548 Squadron. Darwin Civil (Australia), June 1945.
Created in December 1943 in order to defend Darwin against the Japanese, No 548 Squadron was in fact created too late; as a consequence, the pilots were idle for almost two years. No victories were claimed, as the squadron's activity was limited to 18 operational sorties... From 1945 onwards, the Spitfires were not repainted any more, so they retained the standard factory-issue Fighter Command camouflage scheme. S/L Glaser was awarded the DFC in 1942 whilst serving with No 234 Sqn.

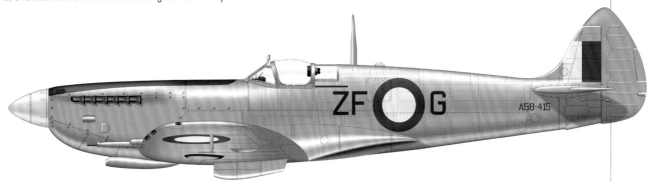

Supermarine Spitfire LF.VIII A58-415. No 549 Squadron. Strauss (Australia), 1944
Created at the same time as No 548 Sqn., No 549 experienced the same lack of combat activity. From mid-1944 onwards, most of the Spitfires used by the squadron were stripped of their paint and left in bare metal, apart from the yellow propeller cone and the small-size numbers and letters.

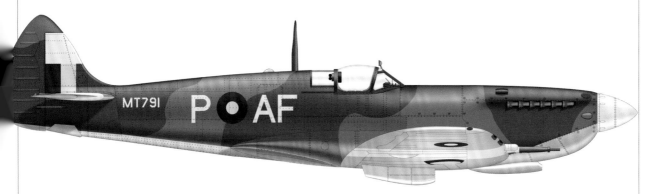

Supermarine Spitfire LF.VIII MT791. No 607 (County of Durham) Squadron. Mingaladon (Burma), summer 1945.
As it was one the three first units to introduce the Spitfire in the Far East in 1943, No 607 Sqn. logically converted to the Mk.VIII in March 1944 at a time when it was fighting the Japanese air Force. At the end of the same year, the squadron started ground attack missions and took part in the liberation of Burma. This did not prevent the squadron from claiming about 15 victories against the Japanese. The squadron was disbanded in August 1945. The plane seen here bears the rapid recognition markings of the region.

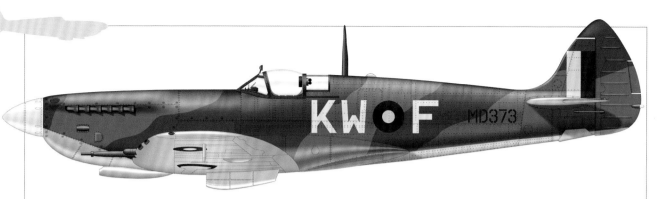

Supermarine Spitfire LF.VIII MD373. No 615 (County of Surrey) Squadron. Palel (India), summer 1944.
No 615 Sqn. was the last of the three fighter units to introduce the Spitfire in India. The squadron swapped its Mk.V for Mk.VIII as late as June 1944. MD373 seen here was one of the first planes of this type to be taken on charge. It was lost on 10 August 1944 with three other Spitfires during a convoy flight towards the squadron's new base. This accident killed four pilots, including the commander of the unit, Australian S/L D. McCormarck, who had been awarded the DFC and Bar. The squadron was based in Calcutta in order to defend the city, but was returned to the front line in early 1945 for ground attack missions, the squadron, therefore, did not claim any victories with the Mk.VIII. The squadron was disbanded in June 1945.

Supermarine Spitfire LF.VIII LV673. No 8 Squadron, IAF, Nidania (India), early 1945.
In July 1944, No 8 Sqn. of the Indian Air Force was the first Indian unit to be equipped with Spitfires. This squadron differed in that it was not originally a Hurricane squadron, but was equipped with the Vultee Vengeance. At first, No 8 Sqn. was made up of a flight of Indian pilots and another of pilots from other Dominions, but when the squadron was deployed in Burma in early 1945, the squadron was mostly an Indian unit. The Indian squadrons had the particularity of only having one individual letter painted on the fuselage. The propellor cone - black and not white - was also a common sight in this unit.

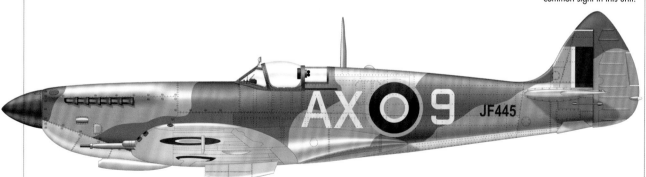

Supermarine Spitfire LF.VIII JF445. Lt David S. Hastie (SAAF). No 1 Squadron, SAAF. Lentini (Italy), September 1943.
This squadron was the first South-African unit to fly Spitfires; it was also the only fighter unit that transferred completely to the Mk.VIII in July 1943. The squadron was also the first SAAF unit to be based outside South Africa. As the introduction of the Mk.VIII into No 1 Sqn. was slow, the squadron had to use the two previous versions for a few weeks. In order to differentiate them easily in flight, the Mk.VIII bore numbers whereas the Mk.V kept their letters. The plane seen here was shot down by Italian Macchi C.202 planes on 3 September 1943. The pilot, Lt Hastie, bailed out of the plane in time and survived. No 1 Sqn. claimed around ten victories with the Mk.VIII.

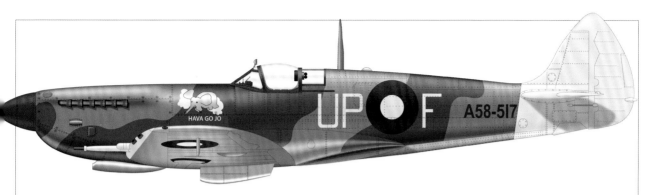

Supermarine Spitfire LF.VIII A58-517. F/O Norman Smithells (RAAF). No 79 Squadron, RAAF. Morotai (Dutch Indies), spring 1945.
No 79 Squadron was the last component of the No 80 Wing to be sent to the Dutch Indies. The squadron converted from the Mk.V to the Mk.VIII in late 1944 and returned to Morotai. Its main mission was that of ground attack. More than 1,300 sorties were flown up to the end of the war, and three planes were lost in action.

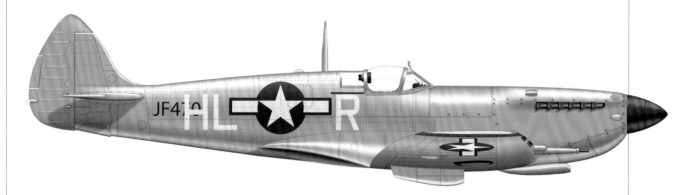

Supermarine Spitfire LF.VIII JF470. 308th FS, 31st FG of the USAAF. Italy 1944.
In the Mediterranean, the British only supplied the Americans with a few Mk.VIII, as a limited amount of that mark were sent to the region. Therefore, when it was time to replace the Mk.V, only the 308th FS received the Mk.VIII, whereas the five other American squadrons were issued with the Mk.IX (or simply retained the Mk.V), even though some Mk.VIII were shared with other units. From spring 1944 onwards, the 308th FS claimed about forty victories with the Mk.VIII. JF470 was one of the few Spitfires to be retained and used as an everyday aircraft after the 31st FG's conversion to Mustangs.

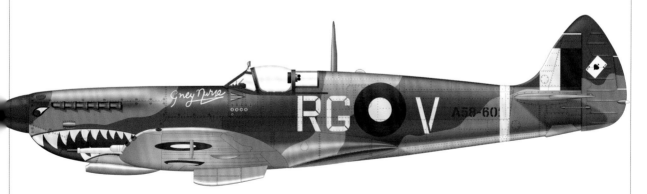

Supermarine Spitfire HF.VIII A58-602. W/C Robert H.M. Gibbes (RAAF). No 80 (Fighter) Wing, RAAF. Morotai (Dutch Indies), spring 1945.
Robert Gibbes was an pre-war RAAF officer. He was sent to the Far East in 1941 with the Australian Nos 450 and 3 Squadrons; he was commander of the latter between February 1942 and April 1943. With a dozen victories claimed in the desert, he was at that time, along with Clive Caldwell, one the great Australian fighter pilots. Gibbes was attached to No 80 Wing upon its creation in order to assist Caldwell. He left in April 1945. As a Wing Commander, Gibbes could chose his code, and opted for "RG", his initials, whereas he had chosen "V" as an individual letter when he fought in the desert. The ace of diamonds was the non-official insignia that No 80 Wing bore in the last weeks of the war. The "Grey Nurse" nickname, which refers to a breed of shark, and the shark's mouth, refer to the unofficial insignia of No 457 Sqn. in 1945, a unit which was in charge of maintaining Gibbes' plane.

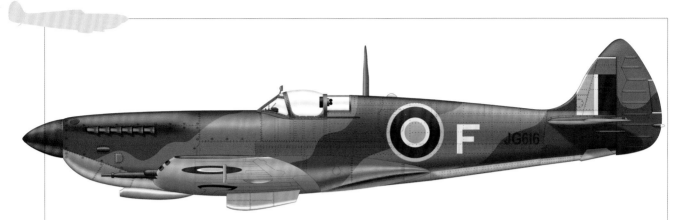

Supermarine Spitfire LF.VIII JG616. Lt-Col Andrew C. Bosman, (SAAF). No 7 Wing, SAAF. Trigno (Italy), spring 1944.
Andrew Bosman was one of the best-known South-African fighter pilots. He was a pre-war SAAF officer and was deployed in the desert from 1941 to 1942, a period during which he showed his extraordinary skills. He returned to the desert for a second tour of operations in January 1944 and was promoted to second in command of the South-African No 7 Wing. He chose a Spitfire Mk.VIII as his personal plane; the plane had clipped wings, which is rare for a Mk.VIII. Even though he could have had his initials as the fuselage code, he chose the letter F, which had been his lucky letter in the desert. He claimed his last two victories with this plane on 27 May 1944.

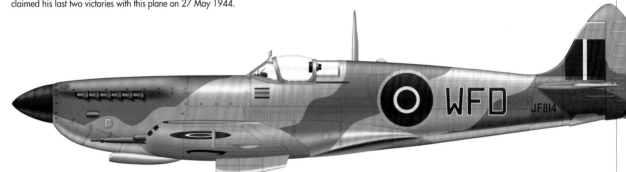

Supermarine Spitfire LF.VIII JF814. AVM William F. Dickson. Desert Air Force, 1944.
William F. Dickson served in the Royal Naval Air Service during the Great War and was awarded the DSO in 1918. He continued his career with the RAF after the war. In 1938, he was already serving in headquarters as Wing Commander. In April 1944, he was given the command of the Desert Air Force, a post he kept until December. After the war, he became the RAF Chief of Staff. As commander of the DAF, he chose JF814 as his personal plane and had it painted with his initials and the Air-Vice Marshall's pennant. It is worth noting the clipped wings.

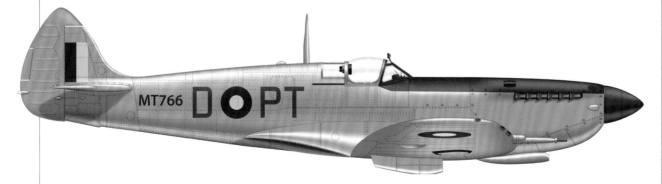

Supermarine Spitfire Mk.VIII MT766. No 1 (Indian) SFTS. Ambala, India, 1945.
The MT766 was a Mk.VIII that served under the No 81 Sqn. At the squadron's disbanding in June 1945, the aircraft was sent to the No 1 Service Flying Training School as it used a great variety of planes, including Spitfires. The MT766, left in bare metal, probably belonged to one of the instructors.

IN COMBAT

In 1942, the situation of Fighter Command had not evolved. Since the previous year, its squadrons had gone onto the offensive and the arrival of the Mk.IX did not in any way change the missions of the pilots who had settled into a sort of routine since the beginning of 1941. What they did with their Mk.V they continued to do with the Mk.IX. It was No 64 Squadron based at Hornchurch which first received the Mk.IX during the course of the summer of 1942. The first kills were claimed as early as mid-day 30 July by F/L Donald E. Kingaby, followed by the destruction of four enemy planes in the evening. S/L W. G. Smith, commanding No 64, was also the first to claim twin kills during this mission.

With the Fighter Command and the 2 TAF

However, the beginnings of the Mk.IX were not especially easy. Indeed, they took part in Operation Jubilee (the Dieppe raid) on 19 August 1942. At this time, three other units had been equipped with the Mk.IX - No 611 Sqn and the Canadian Nos 401 and 402 squadrons – although sometimes partially as the

number of Mk.IX was not always sufficient to totally re-equip a unit. The Mk.IX would suffer several reverses during the course of the first two months of operations, to such an extent that the Luftwaffe shot down forty planes of this type.

Fighter Command experienced one of its worst days on 26 September 1942 when it lost eleven Mk.IX of No 133 (Eagle) Sqn over France. No 133 Sqn had just been transformed after the failed Dieppe raid. Wishing to please the Americans, the British had chosen to transform the three American volunteer units (Nos 71, 131 and 133 Sqns) equipped with the Mk.V, onto the

Above.
Mk IX serial MH869 from the No 302 (« Poznan ») Squadron. (US NARA)

Bottom.
No 127 Sqn. was the first to use the Spitfire Mk.XVI in combat as it flew this type on its first sorties on 8 November 1944. No 66, 229, 403 (RCAF), 416 (RCAF), 421 (RCAF), 453 (RAAF) and 602 Squadrons - all units formerly using the Mk.IX - followed suit at the end of the year. The transition was immediate.

23

No 402 Sqn. Canadian was one of the first fighter units to take on charge the Spitfire Mk.IX. However, the start was somewhat difficult for this version and the first results were mixed, with more losses than victories against the Luftwaffe. However, the Mk.IX still managed to achieve a balance, although it did not succeed in gaining superiority over the Luftwaffe, at least initially. BS428 is seen here during trials, with a bomb attached to the belly.

Mk.IX, before they were transferred to the USAAF at the end of September 1942. No 133 had been chosen as the first squadron to be re-equipped. Although these losses can be partially attributed to worse than forecast weather and bad luck, they nevertheless forced the British to reconsider this decision and finally the three American units were transferred to the USAAF along with their Mk.V, thus allowing the precious Mk.IX to be conserved for RAF units. However, the majority of RAF pilots continued fighting back as well as they could with their Mk.V against the formidable Fw 190.

The losses suffered by No 133 Sqn join those of the first two months of operations and were not compensated by a high number of kills, totalling only thirty, ten of which were claimed over Dieppe.

The beginnings of the Mk.IX were therefore mixed. In the meantime, the Mk.VI had slowly begun to appear, at first with No 616 Sqn in April, followed in July by No 124. The first sorties were flown in May but were restricted to a somewhat defensive role. It was not until July 1942 that the first kill was claimed, a probable Fw 190 on 13 July by an Australian pilot serving in the RAF, F/L Frederick Gaze. Other kills were claimed in the following weeks

and the Mk.V also took part in Operation Jubilee providing high altitude cover for the RAF aircraft involved. F/L Gaze claimed another kill there on that day.

No 124 also opened its tally sheet with the Mk.VI over Dieppe and in a brilliant manner with four confirmed kills and two other probables. However, the Mk.VI also began to disappoint with its unreliable pressurisation system, and pilots also found it uncomfortable to fly. At this time, the Mk.VI's days were numbered. The arrival of the Mk.VII in 1943 resolved most of the problems encountered with the Mk.VI, but this version also had a low-key

An entire complement of Spitfires Mk. IXC of No. 485 (New Zealand) Squadron lined up at the USAAF Station 112 Bovingdon in Hertfordshire on 30 March 1944. *(US NARA)*

career due to the Germans rarely entering British airspace from 1943 onwards.

Recently transformed to the Mk.VII, it was a No 124 Sqn pilot, F/O D. E. Willis, who claimed a kill against a reconnaissance Fw 190 on 15 May 1943.

1942 was, therefore, a difficult year with the disappointment caused by the Mk.VI and difficult beginnings of the Mk.IX. However, the pilots were unanimous in stating that the Mk.IX allowed them to confront the Fw 190 with a certain sense of equanimity as they were perfectly aware that they had a fighter that allowed them to fight on equal terms the formidable German fighter.

Therefore, every unit requested the Mk.IX, but Rolls Royce was unable to supply enough engines and the Mk.IX were sent in priority to the units flying with the 11 and 12 Groups. When these units left for rest periods, they left their Mk.IX to pilots who replaced them and flew Mk.V Spitfires from their bases behind the frontline. This situation would continue until the summer of 1944 when the number of Mk.IX was finally sufficient. When the 2nd Tactical Air Force (2 TAF) was created in June 1943 the Fighter Command strength began to melt away and its influence decreased as that of 2 TAF grew. Fighter Command was renamed ADGB (Air Defence of Great Britain) in November 1943, thus making this transformation official.

At the time of the Normandy landings, the ADGB only had 27 Spitfire squadrons, two with the Mk.VII (Nos 131 and 616) and seven with the Mk.IX (Nos 1, 33, 74, 126, 127, 165 and 501) concentrated, of course, near the future combat zones, that is to say, within 10 and 11 Groups. In 1943 and 1944, Fighter Command and ADGB became more of a defensive force and this made itself felt with the number of kills which decreased, whereas those of the 2 TAF increased and the USAAF grew in strength. The weight of the war in the air no longer rested on the shoulders of the RAF and the roles, and kills, were shared. The role of the ADGB during the first phases of the landings was to fend off any potential Luftwaffe attack against British territory. To this end, the Spitfire squadrons saw limited action, only flying a few offensive sorties from time to time. Only one kill was claimed on D-Day by No 165 Sqn against a Ju 88, followed by only ten more after the landings, and finally none in 1945.

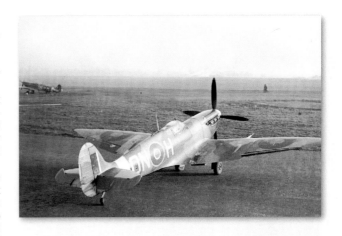

Above.
Spitfire Mark VI serial BR579 of No 124 Squadron RAF, parked in a dispersal at North Weald, Essex. (IWM)
Top.
Spitfire F Mark XVI serial MK850, at the Aeroplane and Armament Experimental Establishment, Boscombe Down, Wiltshire. Originally a Mark IX, this aircraft was converted to Mark XVI standard by installing a Packard Merlin 266 engine, and remained as a test aircraft with the A&AEE. (IWM)

25

It is true that at this time, the Luftwaffe was based far away and that long-range escort missions were attributed as priority to units flying with the Mustang III. The last aerial victories for the Mk.IX were over Arhnem, Holland, during Operation Market Garden (two Bf 109 claimed by New Zealand Wing Commander John Checkett and F/L K. C. M. Gidding of No 118 Sqn). On the other hand, these squadrons returned to their initial role when the first V1 flying bombs were launched against Great Britain. The Spitfire Mk.IX was of course engaged in this new type of air warfare, but its performance no longer allowed it to gain the upper hand. Although approximately 120 V1 flying bombs were destroyed by the Spitfire Mk.IX pilots, this was nothing compared to the Tempest (850 V1) or even the Spitfires equipped with Griffon engines (380 V1).

Towards the end of the war, the Mk.IX, and above all the Mk.XVI, attacked the V2 launch sites present along the European coastline, this being the last great mission for the Merlin powered Spitfires based in Great Britain and where the only danger came from flak.

If there is a second period where one might measure the importance of the Spitfire during the course of the war after the

Above from left to right.
Even though many pilots became aces on the Spitfire Mk.IX, some, and not the least, did not survive their last dogfight. This was the case with Henry W. "Wally" McLeod, a Canadian pilot who was killed in a mission above Arhnem as he was leading No 443 (RCAF) Sqn on 24 September 1944. This Malta veteran (where he scored a total of fifteen victories), took command of No 443 Sqn. upon its creation in spring 1944. Whilst leading this squadron, he scored eight confirmed victories between 19 April and 30 April 1944.

Another "Johnnie", a New-Zealander named John A. Houlton of the No 485 (NZ) Sqn. He fought during the siege of Malta in 1942, and was subsequently sent to this squadron in early 1943. His first confirmed D-Day victory came on 6 June 1944. He ended the war with a score of seven confirmed victories, two of which were shared. *(Paul Sortehaug)*

In 1943, Fighter Command and the 2 TAF were undergoing great changes. New leaders emerged such as Wing Commander John R. Ratten. Even though he is not the highest scoring Australian pilot, he took command of the Hornchurch Wing in May 1943, becoming the first Australian volunteer to take the lead of a Spitfire Wing. He did not survive the War as he was killed by a lung infection in February 1945.

Bottom.
The Spitfire would finally gain ascendency in 1943-44 and during the Normandy landings, it was the most commonly used fighter within the 2 TAF, painted with the famous invasion stripes that became so familiar over Normandy. Seen here is a plane belonging to No 453 Sqn. (Australian) ready to take off with a belly fuel tank. This squadron, which at the time was stationed at Ford near Portsmouth, was the only Australian day fighter squadron present on British soil.

Commander Jacques Schloesing was killed in August 1944. This pilot who was at the head of the No 341 "Free French" Sqn., equipped with the Spitfire Mk.IX, epitomised the pilots of the Free French fighter units. He enlisted as early as June 1940 in the FAFL, where he served in various RAF fighter units before joining No 340 (Free French) Sqn., of which he became commander in early 1943. A few weeks later, he was shot down in flames above occupied France, but managed to return to Great Britain despite suffering from severe injuries. After multiple operations, he was allowed to re-enter active service. He took command of No 341 Sqn. on 24 August 1944, and was at the heart of the fighting two days later. The class of 1950 of the French Ecole de l'Air - an institution for the training of French air force officers - was named after him.

Battle of Britain, it is probably its participation in operations carried out within the 2nd Tactical Air Force, that is to say the air arm of the British Empire forces for the Normandy landings. Created in June 1943, it grouped together a force of fighters, fighter-bombers, reconnaissance aircraft and medium bombers, forming itself around Bomber Command 2 Group which was alone in continuing daylight bombing. In the months that followed, several dozen units were attached and the 2 TAF, as it was planned for the landings, was ready by the end of spring 1944. During that time, it was engaged in dealing with objectives on the continent that were directly linked to the landings, but it

was still not used to the maximum of its capabilities or possibilities. In June 1944, it had thirty squadrons flying with the Spitfire Mk.IX (plus another with the Mk.VII), whereas the ADGB, kept in reserve and mainly tasked with defensive missions, only had twelve squadrons of Spitfire Mk.VII—two—or Mk.IX. The 2 TAF had taken away so many Fighter Command/ADGB squadrons that the Spitfire Mk.IX had become the most used and most versatile version within this tactical air force which comprised of, alongside the Spitfire squadrons, two-dozen other units flying the Typhoon, Mustang or Tempest.

With freshly painted invasion stripes that are so well known

Top right side.
During the Battle of Normandy, many pilots using the Spitfire Mk.IX distinguished themselves in aerial combat. Among them was Wing Commander James E. "Johnnie" Johnson, who scored nine victories between 6 June and 23 August 1944, the three quarters of which whilst flying the Mk.IX. In 1945, this ace had the biggest tally of the RAF.

Opposite.
The South-Africans contributed strongly to the Commonwealth forces that were present in Italy in 1944 and 1945, since a certain number of Spitfire MkVIII or Mk.IX squadrons were sent there. No 1 Squadron of the SAAF was the best performing fighter unit with 165,5 confirmed victories and 26 probables. Seen here are three pilots of that squadron: Captain Stewart A. Finney (left), Major Hannes Faure, an ace who commanded the unit at the time (centre) and Captain Gordon B. Lipawsky (right). By the end of the war, Finney and Lypawsky had both commanded a SAAF squadron.

today, the Spitfire Mk.IX began its assault on fortress Europe in the early hours of 6 June 1944. The initial Luftwaffe reaction was low-key and it was only in the afternoon that the first enemy planes were shot down by No 485 Sqn (New Zealand) and No 349 Sqn (Belgian) which cut to pieces the Ju 88 heavy fighters flying in from Brittany to attack the invasion fleet. It was the New Zealand pilot F/O J. A. Houlton who scored the first official kill in this phase of the war which would end with the liberation of Europe. The Spitfires were again successful a few days later as they were the first planes to land on liberated soil. Indeed, at dawn on 13 June, the Canadians of 126 and 127 Wings landed on two newly-made airstrips, respectively known as B-2 and B-3. Even though they departed for Great Britain that evening, due to a lack of infrastructure, it was of symbolic value as it had been four years since RAF planes had landed in France.

The Luftwaffe took a long time reorganising and attempting to hit back at the Allies, and this explains the relatively few kills in the first days of the landings. The Spitfires did not remain inac-tive though and played an active role in attacking German-held positions. With the Battle of Normandy taking shape and the Germans bringing up more reinforcements, the aerial fighting became both more frequent and intense. During the Battle of Normandy, which ended in late August, the Spitfire IX of the 2 TAF claimed the destruction, confirmed or probable, of approxi-mately 350 German planes. Several German aces fell victim to the Spitfire pilots, such as Hauptmann Josef Wurmheller, with a tally of 102 kills, who lost his fight against the Spitfires of No 441 Sqn (Canadian). Among the pilots who particularly shone at this time was W/C James E. 'Johnnie' Johnson who claimed ten of his thirty-four confirmed kills during this first phase of the landings. However, this success came at a price. Thus, 250 Spitfire Mk.IX were lost during this period. However, many of these planes were shot down by flak which proved itself to be particularly deadly and efficient. Indeed, during the summer of 1944, the Spitfire was the standard 2 TAF fighter-bomber and was used for dive-bom-bing, a technique that the Spitfire pilots soon learned to master.

Opposite.
Since it was used in missions ground attack missions, the Flak inflicted more losses to the Spitfire Mk.XVI than the Luftwaffe fighters did. 127 Squadron Leader Otto Smik was among the first to be killed. The Slovakian pilot was in the midst of his second tour of operations when he was shot down and killed on 28 November 1944. He had already been shot down in early September 1944, but managed to return to Great Britain six weeks later. At the time of his death, his tally of kills was a total of ten confirmed kills, some of which were shared, plus three V1 flying bombs. _(Pavel Vancata)_

Opposite, right.
Peter M. Brothers scored his 16th and final victory with a Spitfire Mk.VII on 7 August 1944. He was in command of the Culmhead Wing, which regrouped the units using the Spitfire Mk.VII, a model that was, at the time, fighting its last weeks of battle. Brothers' victory, as well as the two victories obtained by two pilots of No 131 Sqn. were the last victories attributed to pilots flying with the Mk.VII. Brothers continued his career after the war, rising to the rank of Air Commodore and retiring in 1973.

However, the Spitfire Mk.IX reached its limits during this campaign, suffering from a real lack of firepower, especially when compared to other planes in service, either within the 2 TAF or its American equivalent, the 9th AF. Still armed with two 20 mm cannons and four .303 machine-guns, these small calibre guns were totally obsolete in 1944 for a fighter aircraft and the firepower of the Spitfire was much less than that of the Typhoon, Mustang or Tempest in service with the RAF at that time. Indeed, these aircraft were equipped with either four 20 mm cannons, or six .50 calibre machine-guns that were much more effective against ground targets. Supermarine would make up for this deficiency with the arrival, in the autumn, of the Mk.IXE and Mk.XVI equipped with two .50 calibre machine-guns in place of the four .303, versions which would go as a priority to the 2 TAF. Thus, the Spitfire would be more efficient in this role, but the fact that it was not armed with rockets, a formidable weapon and one which was indispensable in the arsenal of any fighter-bomber in 1944, would herald the beginning of the end of the Spitfire as a multipurpose fighter.

At the end of the Battle of Normandy, the RAF underwent a great reorganisation, especially the 2 TAF. The Merlin engine-equipped Spitfire squadrons (Mk.IX and Mk.XVI) remained a powerful force within the 2 TAF up to April 1945, but its importance diminished at that moment in time. Some squadrons were replaced by other types of Spitfire equipped with Griffon engines, or just changed the type of plane, such as Nos 33 and 222 Sqns which changed over to the Tempest. Although 23 squadrons remained with the Spitfire Mk.IX or Mk.XVI—the latter made up half of the strength -,

Below.
In 1943, the Polish were a sizeable force. Meanwhile, some of their squadrons switched to Mustangs in early 1944. During the Normandy landings, only one Spitfire Mk.IX wing remained, No 131, which comprised of No 302, 308 and 317 Squadrons. Seen here is a plane belonging to No 308 Sqn, photographed during the Normandy campaign.

the 2 TAF now fielded thirty squadrons equipped with either Griffon-engined Spitfires, Typhoons or Tempests. The trend had therefore already begun: the Merlin-engined Spitfire was on the decline. Indeed the aerial victories achieved since June 1944 were misleading as the average level of skill of German pilots in 1944 was far from that who had fought over the Channel in 1942 when the Mk.IX entered into service with the RAF.

The last kill claimed by a 2 TAF Spitfire was on 4 May 1945 by two Canadian pilots of No 411 Sqn - F/L D. F. Cambpell and F/O T. L. O'Brien-, against a Heinkel He 111 north-west of Flensberg. Between September 1944 and May 1945, the pilots flying Merlin-equipped Spitfires nevertheless claimed 400 kills. As a comparison, we can add that at the same time, the Griffon-engined Spitfire pilots, who numbered five times less, claimed 200 kills, and that the Tempest pilots (for seven squadrons deployed on the Continent) claimed approximately 350; these two figures confirm once again the decline of the Spitfire Mk.IX.

A few hours after the final victory of a Merlin-engined Spitfire, the 2 TAF also lost its last pilot with this type of aircraft, F/L L. Szczerbinski, of No 317 Sqn (Polish), who was killed whilst attacking a barge off Wilhelmshaven. Despite the start of this decline, the Merlin-engined Spitfire (Mk.IX and Mk.XVI) still played an essential part in the liberation of Europe in 1944-45.

Although the contribution of the Dominions with the first Spitfire versions was relative, it was in fact a phase where they were building their strength. Indeed, the part played by the Dominions really took off with the arrival of the Spitfire Mk.IX, especially with the Canadians. Indeed, although the latter had been somewhat low-key with their Spitfire Mk.V, the Mk.IX would literally take them from the shadows and into the spotlight. In 1942, seven RCAF fighter units based in Great Britain, flew with the Mk.V, Nos 401, 402, 403, 411, 412, 416 and 421 squadrons. Nos 401 and 402 were part of the first Fighter Command units to go over to the Mk.IX, but this was done in an sporadic manner due to the low number of this version available at that time. In the summer of

1944, all flew with the Mk.IX and were joined by three other RCAF units based in Canada and which had previously flown with the Hurricane. These squadrons became operational in spring 1944 with the Mk.IX as Nos 441, 442 and 443 Sqns. These ten units were then attached to the 2 TAF and would soon distinguish themselves by scoring an impressive number of kills: approximately 675 confirmed or probable, the vast majority of which were for the 2 TAF. However, this came at a price and several exceptional pilots were lost, including Wally McLeod, the highest scoring Canadian ace, commanding at that time No 443 Sqn, and who was killed whilst providing air support for Operation Market Garden on 27 September 1944. It should be noted that this unit had already had on its roster a somewhat untypical pilot, the Mexican, Pilot Officer Luis Perez-Gomez who had joined the RCAF and who was the only Mexican pilot to be killed in action (16 June

Above.
The Spitfire Mk.IX became the most used model in the last months of the war in the Mediterranean. There it was used in various roles, such as dogfighting, ground support and tactical reconnaissance.

1944) on the Western Front.

During the course of autumn 1944, four squadrons, (Nos 403, 416, 421 and 443) swapped their Mk.IX for the Mk.XVI and became at the same time fighter-bomber units. Although few kills were claimed with this version, these four Canadian units were part of those flying this type of Spitfire that kept up constant pressure on the German troops.

All of the Canadian units flew approximately 8,000 sorties with

Opposite.
The Spitfire Mk.IX was removed from the front lines in the months following the end of the war and was consequently mostly used for export, but the RAF kept a few examples for its non-combatant units, such as here with the BS346 used by the Empire Flying School, a unit that trained flying instructors and that used a great variety of planes after the war. The BS348 was one of the first Mk.IX to be produced by converting the Mk.V airframes in 1942; it was only in July 1949 that it was removed from the control lists.

the Mk.XVI in six months of fighting (almost half the total number of sorties with this version during the war), despite the bad weather conditions during the winter. Added to these fighter and fighter-bomber units was a reconnaissance squadron, No 414, which took on charge, from August 1944 onwards, the Spitfire Mk.IX equipped with cameras that it used until April 1945 when it replaced them with the Griffon-engined Spitfire FR.XIV. No 414 Sqn was the only unit operating in western Europe to have flown exclusively with the tactical reconnaissance Spitfire, even if a few also served in some other RAF units.

Australia and New Zealand were massively engaged in other theatres of operations or in other branches of military aviation such as bombers. This meant that these two dominions could not increase the number of fighter units present at the time in Great Britain. The Australians had No 453 Sqn which was progressively transformed from the Mk.V to the Mk.IX, starting in March 1943, and passing under the authority of the 2 TAF the following year, thus taking part in the Normandy landings. During the course of this phase of the war, No 453 claimed thirty kills. In the autumn, it left the 2 TAF and was sent to Great Britain where it swapped its Mk.IX for the Mk.XVI with which it specialised in fighter-bomber missions flown from Great Britain, in particular against V2 launch sites. At the beginning of 1945 it was joined by No 451 Squadron which had arrived from Italy and which also swapped its Mk.IX for the Mk.XVI at that time. Their missions remained unchanged

Above.
Sherman tanks move up past a crash-landed Spitfire from the No 412 (RCAF) Squadron, for an attack on Tilly-sur-Seulles, 17 June 1944. *(IWM)*

up to the end of the war, then these units took part in the occupation of Germany where they changed their Merlin-engined Spitfires for those equipped with the Griffon engine.

Although there were two New Zealand fighter units operational in 1942, only one flew with Spitfires, No 485 Sqn, equipped at the time with the Mk.V. Il then logically changing over to the Mk.IX during the summer of 1943. Apart from two months in the winter of 1943-44, where it was temporarily equipped with the Mk.V, it would retain its Mk.IX until the end of the war. Like the Australian No 453 Sqn, it was integrated into the 2 TAF and did not leave it until May 1945. This unit rendered good service and claimed forty kills with this version, before moving on to the Mk.XVI during the summer of 1945 and finally being disbanded in August. However, the New-Zealanders were also present in large numbers within other Spitfire equipped units. Some even became wing commanders and achieved great things whilst leading them, such as William Crawford-Compton (more than twenty confirmed kills).

Of course, the volunteer pilot squadrons followed the same evolution. All were flying with the

Mk.V when transformation to the Mk.IX began. It was the Norwegians who were the first to receive the Mk.IX, as early as October 1942 for No 331 Sqn, followed by No 332 the following month. These two units came under 2 TAF command and were at the frontline until the cessation of hostilities. At that time, the Norwegian squadrons had claimed almost 170 victories, with approximately 120 for No 331, making it one of the best Spitfire Mk.IX units. These two Norwegian squadrons remained under RAF control until November 1945.

The French followed in October 1942 with No 340 Sqn, followed by No 341 Sqn in March 1943. With the arrival of new pilots coming from North Africa, it became possible to create two new Spitfire Mk.IX units, No 329 in February 1944, followed by No 345 which, after having flown for a while with the Mk.V, was finally transformed in September 1944. These four French units ended the war with the Mk.XVI, claiming with these two versions, sixty confirmed or probable kills. These squadrons left the RAF in November 1945.

The Belgians had two combat units based in Great Britain and both were fighter squadrons which moved onto, at a later stage, the Mk.IX: No 350 in December 1943 and No 349 in February 1944. No 350's time with the Mk.IX was short-lived, lasting for only a few weeks, but the unit saw much action and obtained an impressive amount of kills with another Griffon-engined version of the Spitfire. The other unit, No 349 Sqn, also part of the 2 TAF, was used for support missions until the end of the war and all of its final missions were flown with the Mk.XVI. Both units took part in the occupation of Germany and came under Belgian control in October 1946, and the two squadrons flew at this time with the Mk.XVI.

More than 400 Spitfire Mk.VIII were sent to Australia, which permitted the transformation of three fighter units that were already equipped with Spitfires and the equipping of three other units (two RAF and one RAAF). The three Australian units, regrouped within RAAF No 80 Wing, were sent to the Dutch Indies, where the Spitfire Mk.VIII was used in ground attack missions. Seen here are planes belonging to No 457 Sqn. in Morotai, bearing the famous shark mouths.

The Dutch, whose sole fighter unit, No 322 Squadron, was created at a late stage, successively flew with the Mk.IX and Mk.XVI starting from August 1944 onwards and were engaged in ground support missions until May 1945.

The Czechoslovakians formed a Wing of three fighter squadrons equipped with the Mk.V with its component units Nos 310, 312 and 313 Squadrons transforming to the Mk.IX at the beginning of 1944. However, the Czechoslovakians then suffered a serious shortage of manpower which led the RAF to hold them back from combat as much as possible. Even though the three Czechoslovakian units took part in the initial D-Day operations as No 134 (Czech) Wing, the Czechoslovakian pilots were withdrawn from operations at the end of June 1944 and remained that way until the end of the war before going back to their country in August 1945.

The bulk of foreign forces fighting within the RAF was, however, formed by the Poles. In 1943, all of the Polish fighter units (Nos 302, 303, 306, 308, 315, 316 and 317 Squadrons) had at one time or another flown with the Mk.IX. Although these Polish units proved formidable with their Mk.IX Spitfires (almost one-hundred claimed kills), some of them changed over from Spitfires to Mustangs at the beginning of 1944 and only 302, 303, 308 and 317 Sqns retained their Spits at the time of the Normandy landings. In action with the 2 TAF, they followed the allied advance in Europe and starting at the end of 1944, the Mk.IX were progressively exchanged for the Mk.XVI (or even Mustangs for No 303), a change-over which was nearing completion in May 1945. Although Nos 302 and 308 squadrons received their Mk.XVI at a late stage, from February 1945 onwards, they still had enough time to use them intensively, flying approximately 2,000 sorties up to May 1945. Contrary to other foreign volunteers, the Polish units did not return to their country and were disbanded in 1946. The three units flying with the Mk.XVI (Nos 302, 308 and 317 Sqns) at this time then served in Germany as part of the occupation forces.

Under other skies: the overseas operations

The Spitfire arrived in North Africa at the end of spring 1942, but its use was limited until Operation Torch in November 1942. The number of squadrons increased rapidly and had multiplied threefold at the end of 1942, going from three to ten and if we add the two American fighter groups, the 31st and 52nd FG, the Allies had a force of approximately 300 Spitfires in the region. At that time all units were equipped with the Mk.V, the replacement of which by the Mk.VIII, was planned start in spring 1943. However, just as the arrival of the Fw 190 had been a bad surprise over the Channel in 1941, the arrival of this formidable fighter in the Mediterranean would have the same effect. This forced the RAF to rapidly send the Mk.IX to this theatre of operations, even though it had not originally been planned to deploy this version in this part of the world.

The first of these aircraft were taken on charge within units at the beginning of 1943, but these Mk.IX were much needed in Great Britain and only a low number could be dispatched, allowing two units to be re-equipped, 72 and 81 Sqn, although No 92 and the American units also received some. They were reinforced at the end of March 1943 by a Flight comprising of Polish pilots which was integrated into No 145 Sqn and commanded by the well-known Stanislav Skalski, one of the leading Polish fighter pilots.

Below.
In Asia, the Spitfire Mk.VIII replaced the Mk.V very quickly, differing from the Mediterranean theatre, where the Mk.V was used until the end of the war. No 136 Sqn. transformed to the Mk.VIII as early as February 1944 after only three tours of operations with the Mk.V. Seen here is a plane belonging to this unit undergoing maintenance, towards the end of the war. The working conditions of the mechanics were very harsh in this region, with very basic installations.

Opposite.
Whilst No 80 Wing was fighting the Japanese in the Dutch Indies, No 1 (Fighter) Wing, which regrouped RAF No 54, 548 and 549 squadrons, languished near Darwin, waiting for Japanese raids that never came. These three units were almost completely inactive for the last 18 months of the war when they could have been used elsewhere. Seen here is a plane belonging to No 548 Sqn., a unit created in November 1943 and equipped with the Spitfire Mk.VIII.

These Mk.IX proved very useful, notably during the fighting in Tunisia at that time; the first kill by the RAF with a Mk.IX was claimed by No 72 Sqn on 1 March, with the commander of this unit, S/L Oxspring, sharing the destruction of a Bf 109 with W/O W. Hunter during a mission escorting a tactical reconnaissance aircraft.

Despite their low numbers, approximately 75 kills or probables were claimed by pilots flying the Spitfire Mk.IX up to 13 May, the date on which the Axis forces surrendered in North Africa. 28 of these kills were claimed by Polish pilots who proved to be particularly skilful in this phase of the campaign. This number might appear low but it should be seen in light of the fact that during the same time, that is to say between 1 January and 13 May 1943, a little over 300 victories were claimed by all of the Commonwealth Spitfire units.

With North Africa conquered, the Allies could prepare to take the foot of Europe from the south. The few weeks between the end of the fighting in North Africa and the conquest of Sicily, allowed the RAF to strengthen its units and modernise them. In July, the RAF was able to field fourteen Spitfire fighter squadrons, as well as the six based in Malta which, since the withdrawal of the Luftwaffe and the Regia Aeronautica from the skies over Malta, were somewhat redundant. This would allow these Malta-based units to see some action.

Even though the Mk.IX continued arriving regularly in this theatre of operations, the priority was now given to the 2 TAF in view of D-Day, something which meant that the replacement of ageing Mk.V Spitfires took more time. However, in the interlude, the first Spitfire Mk.VIII arrived in the Mediterranean and during the course of the summer of 1943, four units were totally transformed with this version, Nos 92, 145, and 417 (Canadian) and the South African No 1 Sqn. These units were the only ones to be exclusively equipped with this version, with other RAF squadrons using a few in their roster up to the end of the war. It was not uncommon at this time to see these Mk.VIII flying alongside other Spitfire versions on operations, such as the Mk.V and Mk.IX. The Mk.VIII was in action long enough to take part in the final phases of the invasion of Sicily. It was a South African pilot of No 1 Sqn, Capt J.T. Seccombe, who claimed the first kill with this version

Below.
A general view of the Spitfire Mk.VIII from the No. 452 (RAAF) Squadron dispersal area on Sepingang Airstrip, Balikpapan area. 5 August 1945. *(US NARA)*

on 10 August 1943 when he was based on the island, shooting down a Fw 190. No 145 opened its tally sheet five days later with two kills claimed by Canadian pilots, F/L W. J. Whitside and F/O J. K. Carswell. The latter did not return from this mission and was the first Spitfire Mk.VIII to be killed in a dogfight.

In the weeks that followed, the Spitfire units took part in the invasion of Italy and Mk.VIII found itself at the forefront of the fighting, generally reserved for escort missions due to its better performances compared to the Mk.V. Up to the spring of 1944, the Commonwealth pilots flying with the Mk.VIII claimed almost all of the Spitfire kills. The peak was achieved when covering the Anzio bridgehead between January and June 1944. During the course of these five months, the Spitfire Mk.VIII pilots claimed the bulk of their kills (more than 80), being reinforced at that time by the Mk.IX which claimed a further twenty kills.

This was, however, the swansong of the Mk.VIII, and this was due to two reasons. Firstly, because since the end of 1943, the military planners were looking more towards the Far East and deliveries of the Mk.VIII were sent in priority to this part of the world. This did not mean that the fighter squadrons were not upgraded as the Mk.IX was being produced in large quantities at the time, allowing the RAF to dispatch enough of this Spitfire version from the summer of 1944 onwards. The second reason was due to the Luftwaffe leaving Italy after the fall of Rome in June 1944, and the Normandy landings, as well as the fact that Germany was under ever-increasing air attack, meaning that they had to muster as many aircraft as possible for home defence. The Luftwaffe's objective in Italy thus became one of containing the Allies with very few aircraft.

Even during the course of the landings in Provence (Operation Dragoon), the Luftwaffe was hardly seen and, therefore, only a low number of kills was claimed over Italy between autumn 1944 and spring 1945. The Spitfire was then almost exclusively used as a tactical support aircraft, not just over Italy but also in the Balkans or Greece. Twenty kills with the Mk.VIII or Mk.IX were claimed during this period by other Commonwealth units, with the last kill by a Spitfire of this type being claimed by the Canadian pilot, P/O Norman Pearce, of No 73 Sqn who, with his Mk.IX, shot down a Bf 109 over Yugoslavia on 2 April 1945 whilst returning from a ground-attack mission.

To this can be added fifteen kills by French units integrated into the RAF and which advanced up France from the south. Indeed, a French Wing comprising of three fighter units (326, 327 and 328 Sqns) had been reformed using French Armée de l'Air units after Operation Torch. They were initially equipped with the Mk.V (a version that was progressively changed in mid-1944) and a few Mk.IX, but they finally only had Mk.IX and a few Mk.VIII. They operated from French soil from September 1944 onwards, following the Provence landings and were integrated into the 1 TAF which mostly comprised of USAAF units. Advancing up the Rhone valley, these squadrons arrived in the Alsace, near the German border, at the end of 1944 and ended the war in Germany.

Squadron Leader Arthur Birch from the No 452 (RAAF) Squadron photographed beside his Mk.VIII at Morotai in 1945. *(SDASM)*

SPITFIRE MK.VII TO MK.XVI
COMMONWEALTH SQUADRONS

Spitfire Mk.VII units on 1 July 1944:
Nos 124, 131, 616 Squadrons

Spitfire Mk.VIII units on 1 June 1945:
• In the Far East: Nos 17, 67, 81, 136, 152, 155, 273, 607, 615, 8 (IAF) Squadrons.
• In the Mediterranean: Nos 92, 145, 238*, 241*, 417 (RCAF), 1 (SAAF) Squadrons.
• In the Pacific: Nos 79 (RAAF), 54, 548, 549, 452 (RAAF), 457 (RAAF) Squadrons.

Spitfire Mk.IX units on 1 July 1944:
• In Europe: Nos 1, 16*, 33, 56, 64, 66, 74, 80, 118, 126, 127, 132, 222, 229, 274, 302 (Polish), 303 (Polish), 308 (Polish), 310 (Czech), 312 (Czech), 313 (Czech), 316 (Polish), 331 (Norwegian), 332 (Norwegian), 340 (French), 341 (French), 345 (French), 349 (Belgian), 401 (RCAF), 402 (RCAF), 403 (RCAF), 411 (RCAF), 412 (RCAF), 416 (RCAF), 421 (RCAF), 441 (RCAF), 442 (RCAF), 443 (RCAF), 453 (RAAF), 485 (NZ), 501, 602, 611 Squadrons.
• In the Mediterranean: Nos 32, 43, 72, 73, 87, 93, 94, 111, 185, 208, 225*, 238*, 241*, 242, 243, 256*, 451 (RAAF), 601, 680*, 1435, 2 SAAF, 3 SAAF, 4 SAAF, 7 SAAF, 40 SAAF, 41 SAAF Squadrons.

Spitfire Mk.IX units on 1 January 1947:
Nos 32, 43, 73, 111, 208, 225, 253 Squadrons.

Spitfire Mk.XVI on 1 June 1945:
Nos 287*, 288*, 289*, 302 (Polish), 308 (Polish), 316 (Polish), 322 (Dutch), 329 (French), 340 (French), 341 (French), 345 (French), 349 (Belgian), 403 (RCAF), 411 (RCAF), 412 (RCAF), 416 (RCAF), 421 (RCAF), 443 (RCAF), 451 (RAAF), 453 (RAAF), 485 (NZ), 603 Squadrons.

Sptifire Mk.XVI units on 1 January 1950:
Nos 5, 17, 20, 604, 609, 612 Squadrons.

deployed their Nos 2, 3, 4 and 7 Squadrons equipped with the Spitfire Mk.IX, thus making a major contribution to the allied war effort in the Mediterranean. The Poles were also present with No 318 Sqn, a tactical reconnaissance unit that used the Mk.IX from November 1944 onwards, alongside the Mk.V. The Mk.IX became the standard RAF tactical reconnaissance plane in this theatre of operations and Nos 208 and 225 Squadrons also used the reconnaissance Mk.IX from 1944 onwards, as well as the South African 40 and 41 Sqns, even though the latter was disbanded in November of the same year. This transformation was started because the RAF could not always use its Mustang I which were deployed at the time with the 2 TAF. It fell to the Spitfire, therefore, to carry out this essential role and it was one that it accomplished honourably. The French did the same within another reconnaissance unit, GR 2/33, which served with the 1 TAF.

Thus, in 1945, even though the Mk.V was still in service, the Mk.IX was very much in the majority within Spitfire units. Of course, pilots distinguished themselves whilst flying this plane, the first of these being the highest scoring Mediterranean ace, Neville Duke, who achieved his eight kills with the Mk.IX or Mk.VIII. But other aces, such as New-Zealander Evan Mackie or the RAF American pilot Lace Wade, also put their Mk.IX or Mk.VIII to good use in order to increase their tally of kills.

The other major force in the region, the Americans, also took on charge the Spitfire Mk.VIII and Mk.IX, replacing their Mk.V. They were even initially favoured as, despite the small number of Mk.IX sent to this theatre of operations in 1943, the British did not hesitate in lending them a few instead of their own squadrons. Thus, the 307th FS of the 31st FG flew with the Mk.IX in spring 1943, the 308th FS of the same group used the Mk.V and a few Mk.VIII, and the 309th the Mk.VIII. The 31st FG was followed by the 52nd FG (2nd, 4th and 5th FS) during the course of the summer. The Americans used the Spitfire until April 1944 and it was at this time that their fighter groups changed over to American aircraft with the surviving Spitfires being handed back to the British. Even though it is difficult to know the precise number of Spitfires used by these two American fighter groups, we believe that the number is around fifty Mk.VIII and 120 Mk.IX. The American pilots equipped with the Mk.VIII or Mk.IX claimed approximately 125 kills for the 31st FG (approximately 35 of which were for the 309th FS and its Mk.VIII) and fifty for the 52nd FG respectively.

The French were not the only ones to contribute to the war effort in this area. The Canadians of No 417 Sqn, the sole RCAF unit present in the Mediterranean, claimed thirty kills with their Mk.VIII Spitfires between October 1943 and May 1944, commanded by the ace, Albert Houle. This squadron was reinforced by an Australian unit, No 451, which became a fighter unit in 1943, but which departed for Great Britain in October 1944 where it finished the war with the Mk.XVI.

As well as the Mk.VII equipped squadron, the South Africans also

Opposite.
Airmen prepare a Supermarine Spitfire Mark VIII of No 607 (County of Durham) Squadron for a sortie during monsoon conditions at Mingaladon, Burma. *(IWM)*

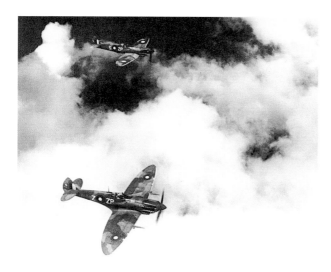

Opposite.
A pair of Spitfires Mk. VIII of No. 457 Squadron RAAF, ZP-Z and ZP-S airborne over Dutch East Indies, 1945. The squadron nicknamed itself the "Grey Nurse Squadron" (after the Australian term for a sand tiger shark) because of the grey-and-green camouflage of their Spitfires Mk. VIII. They also adopted sharkmouth markings on the nose and the uniform "Grey Nurse" logo on the upper cowlings of their aircraft.

Below.
Group Captain Clive "Killer" Caldwell seen at Morotai in 1945, when he was commanding No 80 (Fighter) Wing RAAF. The scoreboard in front of the windscreen of his Spitfire Mk. VIII numbered A58-484 depicts his 27,5 victories against German, Italian and Japanese aircraft which made Caldwell the top Australian ace of the war. *(Air Office)*

The last two confirmed American kills were attributed to Lt Joe H. Blackburn of the 5th FS on 6 April 1944, against two Bf 109s.

Although the Spitfire Mk.IX was extensively used in the Mediterranean, it was, on the other hand, totally absent from the Far-East and the Pacific. The RAF introduced the Spitfire to the Far-East in 1943 with the Mk.V, with these planes being a most welcome reinforcement, claiming dozens of kills within a few weeks. However, the Mk.V began to be replaced at the beginning of 1944 by the Mk.VIII, of which almost half the total production would finally be sent to these theatres of operations. During the course of the first half of 1944, the Mk.VIII did not only replace the Mk.V in the three units it equipped (Nos 136, 607 and 615 Sqns), reinforced by two other units from Italy, Nos 81 and 152, which allowed the re-equipping of other units flying with the Curtiss Mohawk at the time (No 155) or Hurricanes (Nos 17, 67 and 273). Other RAF units were added later (No 132) and Indian Air Force (No 8). When the Mk.VIII arrived in the Far-East, the RAF was in the midst of an offensive and fierce fighting took place until July 1944. After a relatively calm period, a final offensive took place at the end of the same year, ending with the liberation of Rangoon in May 1945. In this period, the Spitfire Mk.VIII pilots claimed fifty kills, especially in 1944, as in 1945 the Japanese considerably reduced their air activity in the region. The final victory in the Far-East was claimed on 29 April by P/O Bob Connell of No 17 Sqn, a unit com-

The maintenance and repair section of No 452 Squadron's Spitfires LF.VIII on Sepingang Airstrip, Balikpapan Area, August 1945. *(US NARA)*

manded at that time by the Battle of Britain ace 'Ginger' Lacey. This victory was also the last for the RAF in this theatre of operations.

After the Mediterranean and the Far-East, the Spitfire left for the Pacific in order to carry on what the Mk.V had already started, that is to say the defence of Australia within the famous 'Churchill Wing', 1 (Fighter) Wing, RAAF. However, the Mk.VIII, of which many made their way to Australia starting from the end of 1943, in fact arrived well after the most critical phases and the threat of Japanese invasion was now no more than a distant memory. The Mk.VIII soon replaced the Mk.V within RAF No 54 Sqn and in Australian Nos 452 and 457 Sqns, soon joined by new units, Nos 548 and 549 Sqns of the RAF and No 79 Sqn of the RAAF. Thus, at the beginning of 1945, there were six squadrons flying with the Mk.VIII, divided into two wings. No 1 Wing, comprising of the three RAF squadrons was allocated the role of defending Darwin and No 80 (Fighter) Wing, grouping together the three Australian units, was sent to New Guinea in a more offensive role of fighting the Japanese, where they were beset with American imposed constraints and restrictions that only ceased at the end of the war. However, the opportunities to shoot down Japanese planes were rare and only a few kills were claimed by the Mk.VIII. The three RAF units of 1 Wing would find themselves plunged into a demoralising period of inactivity due to the fact that no Japanese planes infringed their air space in the final months of the war, indeed 548 and 549 Squadrons combined, flew less than fifty sorties in eighteen months! But, we should also note that 549 Sqn also held the record for the longest distance operational Spitfire mission when half a dozen of its planes were sent on a ground attack mission in June 1945 over East Timora.

Faced with these facts and knowing that more than 150 of the 410 Mk.VIII remained in the Australian depots, we can honestly say that sending the Mk.VIII to the Pacific was in part a waste of both human and material resources and that the Mk.VIII was never able to show what it was capable of in this theatre.

The Spitfire Mk.IX and Mk.XVI were the only versions to continue their careers within the RAF after the war. The RAF was progressively restructured and many squadrons were disbanded wherever the RAF was stationed. These versions were changed for more modern aircraft within operational units, including those with Griffon-engined Spitfires and by 1947, the export Mk.IX were all withdrawn.

The squadrons started their transfer from the Mk.IX to the Mk.XVI from February 1945. When Germany capitulated, No 340, 341 and 345 Squadrons were flying with this type; 2,000 sorties were recorded. Seen here is a plane of No 340 Sqn., bearing the French roundels, which were tolerated at the time by the RAF authorities. (Jacques Mutin).

Above.

The Mk.XVI (or Mk.16, as it was renamed after the war) continued to be used after the war, notably becoming the plane used by the Auxiliary Air Force squadrons, which were reformed after the war and whose had three-letter codes. The TE474 (which bears the its unit code - RAB) was used by No 501 Sqn., then by No 613 Sqn. before being destroyed in an accident in April 1951. This plane bore the insignia of No 501 Sqn. as well as the squadron leader pennant.

The Mk.XVI survived for a few more years as the ideal intermediate aircraft whilst awaiting more modern planes, but its role remained fairly low-key.

The Mk.XVI was also the plane that the Auxiliary Air Force initially used when the latter was reformed after the war. However, the domain where the Mk.XVI was most used between the end of the nineteen-forties and the beginning of the fifties was in advanced flying schools where it helped hundreds of pilots to learn to fly high performance aircraft before joining operational units. The Spitfire was able to still fulfil this role as the RAF had not been totally equipped with jet aircraft. But when the RAF was totally equipped with jet fighters, the Spitfire Mk.XVI was no longer suited to this role and its withdrawal became a necessity. This version was also found at this time within a host of secondary units that were not dedicated to training, not counting the planes of high ranking officers who had fought with the Spitfire during the war.

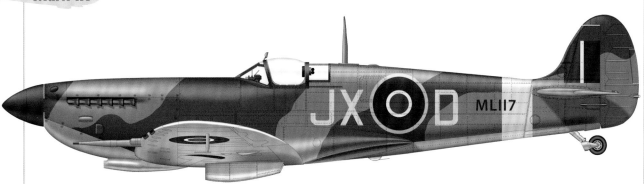

Supermarine Spitfire LF.IX ML117. No 1 Squadron. Manston (Great Britain), early 1945.
No 1 Sqn. was equipped with Spitfires as late as April 1944, as it had previously been using Hurricanes and Typhoons. The squadron received the Mk.IX but was only deployed overseas at the end of the war. Since the squadron was kept away from the fighting, it did not claim any kills with this type, but played an active role in the fight against V1 flying bombs, 40 of which they shot down.

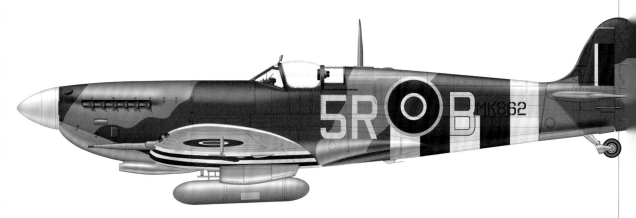

Supermarine Spitfire Mk.IX MK862. No 33 Squadron. Funtington (Great Britain), summer 1944.
No 33 Sqn. fought in the Middle East from the very beginning of the war, but was sent to Great Britain in spring 1944, switching from the Mk.V to the Mk.IX at the same time. The squadron converted to Tempests in December 1944.

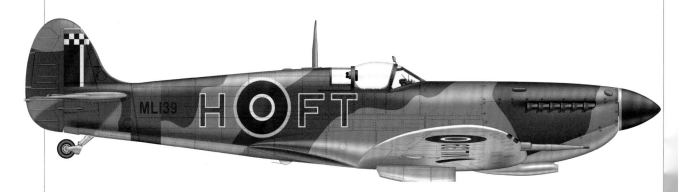

Supermarine Spitfire Mk.IX ML139. No 43 Squadron. Klagenfurt (Austria), summer 1945.
No 43 Sqn., which fought in the Mediterranean, started receiving the Mk.IX in August 1943. By January 1944, the squadron was totally equipped with the Mk.IX. It took part in the capture of the Italian peninsula at the end of the war, undertaking ground attack missions. Once the war was over, the squadron took part in the occupation of Austria.

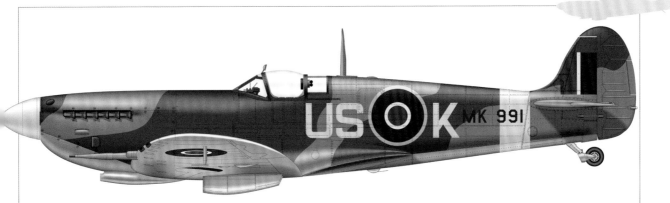

Supermarine Spitfire LF.IX MK991. No 56 (Punjab) Squadron. Newchurch (Great Britain), spring 1944.
No 56 Sqn. had been using Hurricanes and Typhoons when it switched to Spitfires in spring 1944. It received the
Mk.IX, but only used this type for three months, from April to June 1944, before being equipped with Tempests.

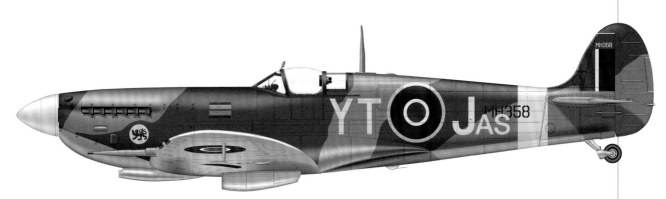

Supermarine Spitfire LF.IX MH358.S/L James E. Storrar. No 65 (East India) Squadron. Kingsnorth (Great Britain), summer 1943.
As it had been using the Mk.I, II and V, switching to the Mk.IX in August 1943 was a logical step for No 65 Sqn. The squadron was led by Squadron
Leader James E. Storrar's at the time, an ace with a dozen victories. With MH358, Storrar claimed two more kills, obtained on 18 August and 18 Sep-
tember respectively; the squadron claimed one more victory with the Mk.IX. Storrar stepped down from commanding the squadron in November, shortly
before No 65 switched to the Mustang III. Storrar's plane, seen here, is painted with the letters JAS, a code usually reserved for Wing Commanders.
Another particularity is the serial number painted in white on the tailplane.

Supermarine Spitfire LF.IXE PT540. S/L Hugh A.S. Johnston. No 66 Squadron. B.33 (Campneuseville), France, summer 1944.
No 66 Sqn., just like No 65, was one of the operational units using Spitfires when war was declared. The squadron stopped using the Mk.V in November 1943 and kept them for a year before converting to the Mk.XVI. The squadron took part in the liberation of Europe with the 2 TAF. In September 1944, the squadron was commanded by S/L H.A.S. Johnston, an ace and a Battle of Malta veteran. PT540 bore the 2 TAF markings that were first
used in September 1944. No 66 Sqn. claimed a dozen victories with the Mk.IX.

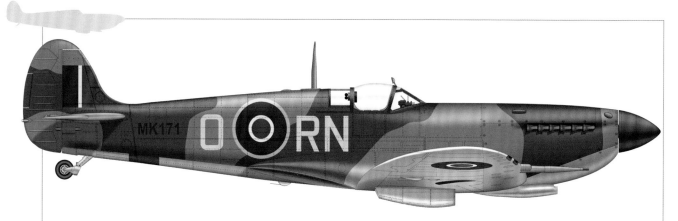

Supermarine Spitfire Mk.IX MK171. No 72 (Basutoland) Squadron. Rimini (Italy), summer 1944.
Towards the end of 1944, No 72 Sqn. was flying ground attack missions in support of allied troops fighting in Italy, but it claimed few aerial victories. The Mk.IX, at that time, was the most widespread version of the Spitfire in this part of the world.

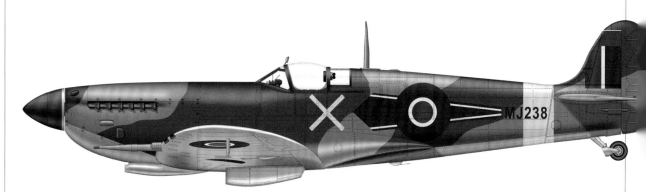

Supermarine Spitfire Mk.IX MJ238. No 73 Squadron. Cannes (France), March 1945.
The No 73 Sqn. began replacing its Mk.V with Mk.IX in October 1943, but its Mk.V planes had only been totally replaced by September 1944. At the time, the squadron had become a fighter bomber unit deployed in Italy and France, but also in Greece (which was under the threat of a civil war) and in Yugoslavia. Towards the end of the war and due to the lack of Luftwaffe activity, No 73 Sqn. began to be repainted with its pre-war markings, which was against the rules at the time; this remained relatively low-key as they only used blue paint. The squadron kept its Mk.IX until November 1947.

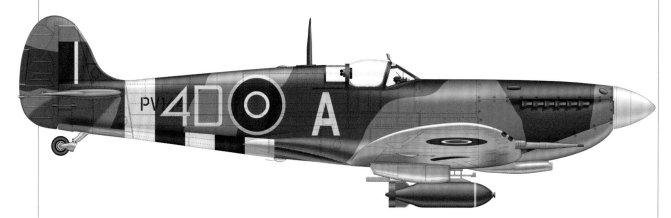

Supermarine Spitfire Mk.IX PV144. S/L J. F. C. Hayter. No 74 (Trinidad) Squadron. B.70/Deurne (Belgium) autumn 1944.
No 74 Sqn., after a brief deployment in the Middle East, returned to the United Kingdom in April 1944, where it was equipped with the Mk.IX for fighter-bomber missions, before joining the 2 TAF on the continent in August of the same year. The squadron flew with the Mk.IX until March 1945 when it changed over to the Mk.XVI. PV144 seen here bears the individual letter A, which was frequently used by squadron commanders.

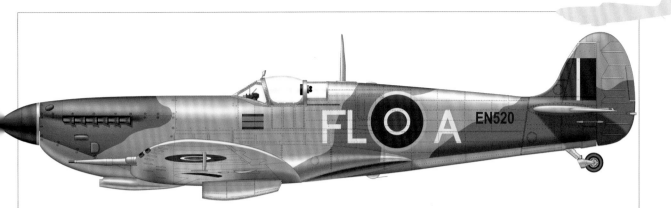

Supermarine Spitfire Mk.IX EN520. S/L Colin Gray (NZ). No 81 Squadron. Bône (Algeria), early 1944.
As No 81 Sqn. was sent to North Africa in November 1942, the squadron was equipped with the Mk.V. In early 1943, the squadron began to progressively issued with the Mk.IX, which had just arrived in this particular theatre of operations. The squadron claimed about thirty victories with the Mk.IX until it was sent to the Far East in November 1943; there, it switched to the Mk.VIII. S/L Gray, a New-Zealander serving for the RAF, chose EN520 as his personal aircraft when he became squadron leader in February 1943. Colin Gray was one of the leading New Zealand fighter pilots and ended the war with 29 confirmed victories to his name, including 2 shared.

Supermarine Spitfire Mk.IXE NH346. S/L G. R. S. McKay. No 87 (United Provinces) Squadron. Pontedera (Italy), April 1945.
No 87 Sqn. started to receive the Mk.IX in June 1943; but, as was often the case in the region, the squadron had to use the Mk.V (and even sometimes the Mk.VIII) at the same time, as the Mk.IX was not delivered in great numbers. In 1944, the situation improved so quickly that by June, the entire squadron was flying with the Mk.IX. The squadron took part in fighter-bomber missions in Italy and Yugoslavia, then in the occupation of Austria, until it was disbanded in December 1946.

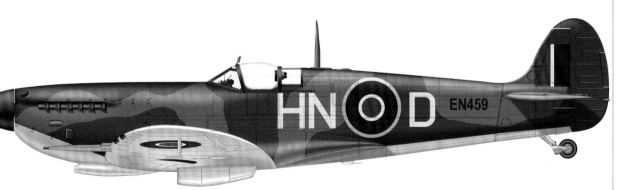

Supermarine Spitfire Mk.IX EN459. F/L Irving F. Kennedy (RCAF). No 93 Squadron. Foggia (Italy), Autumn 1943.
No 93 Sqn. flew with the Mk.IX as well as the Mk.V from 1943 until February 1944. EN459 was the plane with which F/L Kennedy claimed his last Italian victory on 15 October. During this mission, the squadron shot down four Bf 109, using both the Mk.V (two kills) and the Mk.IX (two kills). "Hap" Kennedy returned to Great Britain shortly afterwards and took part in the Normandy landings with Canadian No 401 Sqn., which also used the Mk.IX. He claimed 15 victories during the war, five of which were shared. EN459 seen here has recently been repainted with the Temperate Land Scheme.

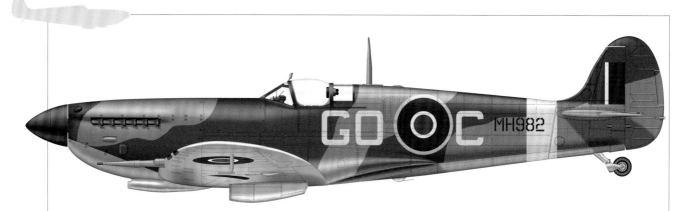

Supermarine Spitfire Mk.IX MH982. No 94 Squadron. Sedes (Greece), spring 1945.
No 94 used both the Mk.V and the Mk.IX until February 1945. At the time, the squadron was supporting the royalists in the Greek civil war. The squadron was disbanded in April 1945. The nose of the plane was painted red, which is rare.

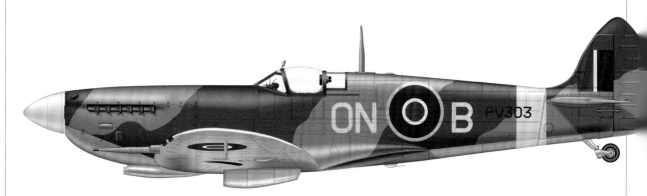

Supermarine Spitfire HF.IX PV303. No 124 (Baroda) Squadron. Coltishall (Great Britain), February 1945.
No 124 Sqn. had been flying with the Mk.VI and VII when it switched to the HF.IX in July 1944. The squadron's missions remained the same though, as they continued to escort bombers flying from Great Britain. In August 1945, the squadron was equipped with Meteors. The plane seen here was sold to Denmark after the war.

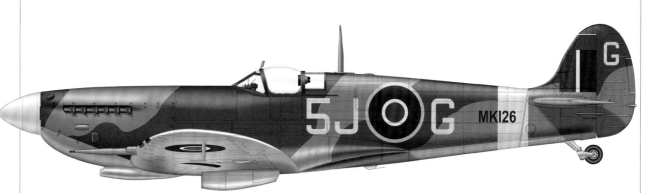

Supermarine Spitfire Mk.IX MK126. No 126 (Persian Gulf) Squadron. Bradwell Bay (Great Britain), autumn 1944.
No 126 Sqn. accomplished remarkable things in Malta. It was entirely converted to the Mk.IX in March 1943, before leaving for Great Britain in April 1944 and subsequently taking part in the Normandy landings. In December, the squadron swapped its Spitfires for Mustangs. The individual letter painted on the tailplane is an unusual marking for an RAF plane.

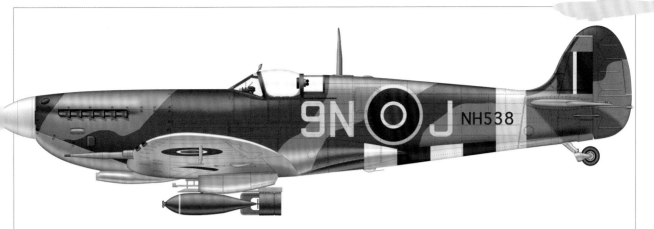

Supermarine Spitfire Mk.IX NH538. No 127 Squadron. B.57/Lille (France), September 1944.
Having used the Mk.V in the Middle East, No 127 Sqn. returned to the United Kingdom in March 1944 in order to join the 2 TAF as a fighter-bomber unit, where it was equipped with the Mk.IX. In November, the squadron switched over to the Mk.XVI.

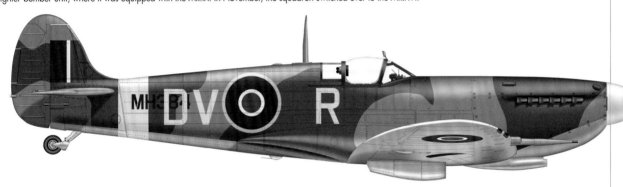

Supermarine Spitfire Mk.IX MH384. No 129 (Mysore) Squadron. Hornchurch (United Kingdom), summer 1943.
Having used the Spitfire right from its creation, No 129 used the Mk.I, Mk.II and Mk.V successively before upgrading to the Mk.IX in June 1943. During the short period in which it used that mark (it switched to the Mustang III in April 1944), the squadron claimed about twenty victories. The squadron's association with the Mk.IX did not end then however, as the squadron went back to that mark at the end of the war when it was based in Norway and where it stayed until 1945. The squadron was disbanded in Great Britain in September 1946. The shape of the letter F and the off-centred R are characteristic of this unit.

Supermarine Spitfire Mk.IX TE215. No 130 (Punjab) Squadron. Odiham (United Kingdom), summer 1946.
No 130 Sqn. had been using Spitfire right from its creation when it swapped its Griffon-engined fighters for the Mk.IX when the squadron was sent to Norway at the end of the war. Like No 129, the squadron returned to the United Kingdom in November 1945 and, in October 1946, became a jet unit when it was issued with Vampires. TE215, with a tear-drop cockpit, was subsequently sold to the SAAF.

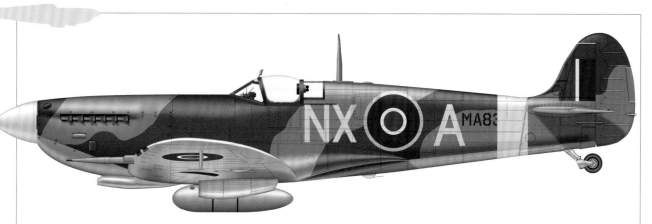

Supermarine Spitfire LF.IX MA834. No 131 (County of Kent) Squadron. Churchstanton (United Kingdom), February 1944.
The No 131 Sqn. was among the rare RAF fighter units to have used all of Spitfire's Merlin-engined models (the Mk.I, II, V, VII, VIII and IX). The Mk.IX was, in fact, just a transitional type used between September 1943 and March 1944, before receiving the Mk.VII.

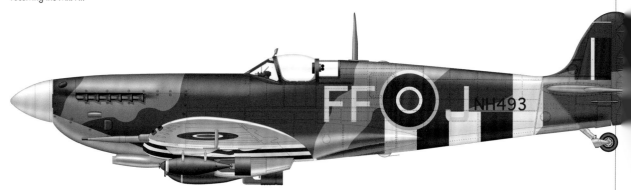

Supermarine Spitfire Mk.IXE NH493. No 132 (City of Bombay) Squadron. W/O Robert C. Harden (RNZAF). B.11/Longues (France), 15 August 1944.
No 132 Sqn., which was also using Spitfires from its creation, went from the Mk.I to the Mk.II and then to the Mk.V (and a few Mk.VI), before taking on charge the Mk.IX from September 1943. In January 1944, the squadron entered the 2 TAF, which it left in September in order to enter the Fighter Command before leaving for the Far East. In Europe, No 132 Sqn. claimed approximately 25 victories with the Mk.IX. NH493, on the other hand, was shot down by flak with its New-Zealander pilot on 15 August 1944.

Supermarine Spitfire Mk.IXB BS294. Pilot Officer Dennis D. Smith (United States). No 133 (Eagle) Squadron. Great Samford, 26 September 1942.
No 133 (Eagle) Sqn. was the last of three units made up of American pilots serving for the RAF or the RCAF to be created. It was also the only unit to take on charge the Mk.IX, and was consequently among the first to be declared operational with this mark. Meanwhile, No 133 was at the origin of one of the biggest tragedies suffered by the Fighter Command when it lost eleven of the thirteen Mk.IX sent on an escort mission on 26 September 1942. Dennis Smith, from Oklahoma, was killed in the crash of his plane on that day. It is worth noting the letter I, which was seldomly used by the RAF fighter units.

Supermarine Spitfire Mk.IXB EN315. No 145 Squadron (Polish Fighter Team), Ben Gardane (Tunisia), May 1943.
In 1943, the Polish sent a dozen pilots to North Africa, placed under the responsibility of No 145 Sqn. These men formed a separate Flight, and their planes, all of which were Mk.IX, were painted with numbers, as letters were used by the squadron's two other Flights. This Polish Flight was led Stanislaw Skalski's, a legendary Polish fighter pilot. "Skalski's Circus", as the unit was often nicknamed, claimed approximately thirty victories in two months of operations. The squadron was disbanded at the end of the Tunisian campaign. The swastikas painted on the fuselage refer to the plane's kills, and not to the pilot's personal victories, as the Flight had more pilots than planes.

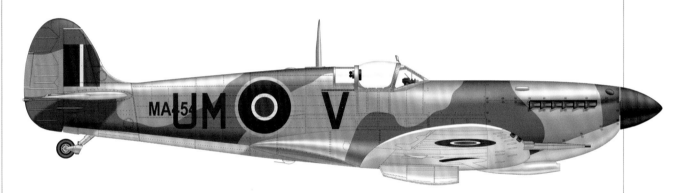

Supermarine Spitfire Mk.IX MA454. F/O R. J. Bell. No 152 (Hyderabad) Squadron. Serretelle (Italy), September 1943.
Before leaving for the Far East in November 1943, No 152 Squadron fought in Italy; in its last weeks there, in September 1943, the squadron took the Mk.IX on charge. The code letters, painted black instead of the usual red, were possibly added to distinguish the Mk.IX from the Mk.V that the squadron used at the same time.

Supermarine Spitfire Mk.IX PL317. No 165 (Ceylon) Squadron. Vaernes (Norway), summer 1945.
No 165 Sqn. was twice equipped with the Spitfire Mk.IX: the first time, between October 1943 and February 1945, when it claimed a dozen victories, and the second time, in June 1945, when it was based in Norway for a few weeks before being sent back to Great Britain where it was disbanded in September 1946. PL317 was destroyed in an accident in Norway on 12 September 1945.

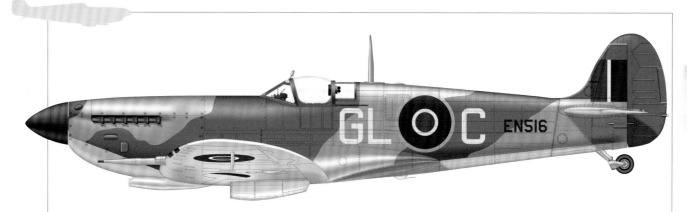

Supermarine Spitfire Mk.IX EN518. No 185 Squadron. Loreto (Italy), spring 1944.
No 185 Sqn. was one of the units in Malta which established its reputation with Spitfires. Once the island was no longer under threat, the squadron was sent to Italy, where it received a few Mk.IX in addition to its Mk.V. The unit only came to be totally equipped with the Mk.IX, as well as a few Mk.VIII, in September 1944. EN518 seen here was one of the first Mk.IX to be sent to the Mediterranean in March 1943, which explains its "desert" camouflage scheme, which was not very well suited to Italian terrain. Indeed, the planes were only repainted with a new scheme during depot inspections. For this reason, in 1943-44, the units often had planes with different camouflage schemes.

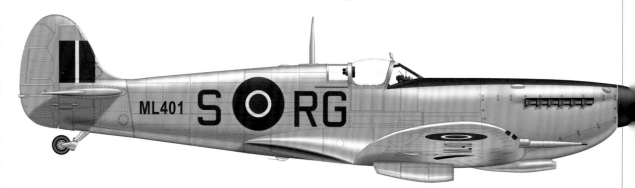

Supermarine Spitfire Mk.IX ML401. No 208 Squadron. Ein Shemer (Palestine), early 1947.
No 208 Sqn. was a tactical reconnaissance unit that used Mk.IX equipped with cameras in the last months of the war. Once peace was restored, the squadron was sent to Palestine, where it was equipped with the Spitfire FR.18. from August 1946 onwards. It gave up its last Mk.IX Spitfires in June 1947. At the time, most of its Mk.IX no longer had camouflage scheme.

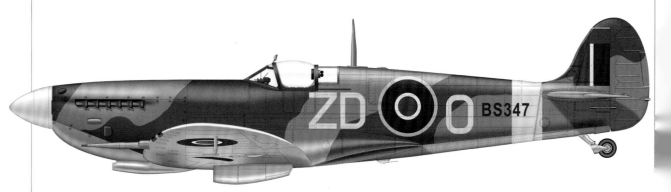

Supermarine Spitfire Mk.IX BS347. No 222 (Natal) Squadron. Hornchurch (United Kingdom), spring 1943.
BS347 was one of the first Mk.IX to be received by No 222 Sqn. which, up to then, had been using the Mk.V. They used the Mk.IX until December 1944 when the squadron converted to the Tempest Mk.V. No 222 claimed around 35 victories with the Spitfire Mk.IX. It is worth noting the letter O, which was rarely used among fighter units.

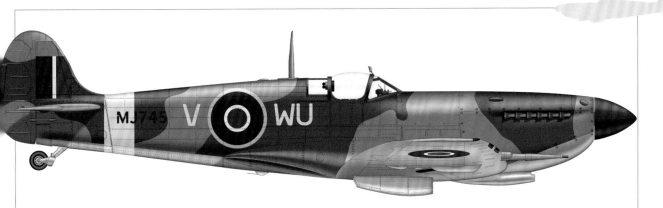

Supermarine Spitfire Mk.IX MJ745. No 225 Squadron. Klagenfurt (Austria), autumn 1945.
No 225 Sqn. was a tactical reconnaissance unit that arrived in North Africa in November 1942 using both Mustangs and Hurricanes. In January 1943, the unit was equipped with the Spitfire Mk.V then, in June 1944, with the Mk.IX. At the time, these planes flew in pairs during missions, with one tasked with taking photos and the other protecting it ("weaver"). After the war, the squadron took part in the occupation of Austria before being disbanded in January 1947. As these planes always flew at low altitude, many of these Spitfire Mk.IX had their wings clipped.

Supermarine Spitfire Mk.IX BS342. No 238 Squadron. El Gamil (Egypt), September 1943.
No 238 Sqn., a Hurricane-equipped fighter unit, was progressively converted to Spitfires starting from January 1943, but only relinquished its last Hurricanes in September when a few Mk.IX were delivered in addition to the Mk.V. BS342 and MA407 (seen below) were among the first planes to be taken on charge, as No 238 Sqn., then based behind the lines, was in charge of air defence in that zone, and therefore had to have planes capable of fulfilling this role at all altitudes. BS342 was then reserved for high-altitude interception missions, which explains its adapted camouflage scheme. In this unit, various markings and camouflage schemes were used together; some planes bore the "KC" code which was attributed to the squadron, or a two-colour tailplane flag, unlike BS342 seen here which has a small "fin flash" with a narrow white stripe in the middle.

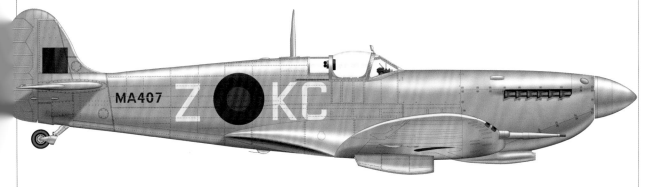

Supermarine Spitfire Mk.IX MA407. No 238 Squadron. El Gamil (Egypt), September 1943.
See BS342 caption.

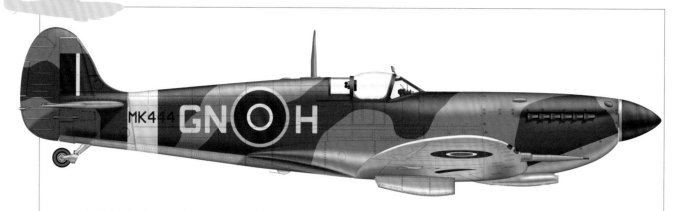

Supermarine Spitfire Mk.IX MK444. No 249 (Gold Coast) Squadron. Prkos (Yugoslavia), spring 1945.
No 249 Sqn., a unit which gained recognition with its exploits in Malta in 1942 where it flew with Spitfires was, at the end of the war, one of the RAF's best fighter units, claiming more than 400 confirmed or probable victories. However, a small number of these victories were achieved with the Mk.IX, a mark that the squadron used briefly in the summer of 1943. The squadron switched to Mustangs in 1944, but used the Mk.IX for a short period of time in April-May 1945.

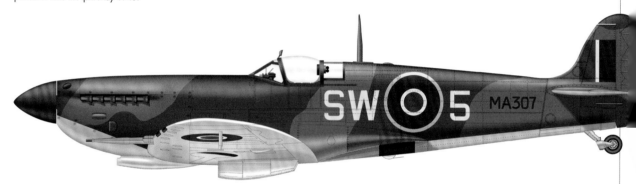

Supermarine Spitfire Mk.IX MA307. No 253 (Hyderabad State) Squadron. Capodichino (Italy), December 1943.
In late 1943, No 253 Sqn. was based in Italy and was equipped with a mix of Mk.V and Mk.IX. In order to differentiate the two models in flight (especially since they did not perform the same), numbers were given to the Mk.IXs. From November 1943, the squadron used the Mk.IX exclusively. The red stripe was probably used occasionally and solely within the squadron.

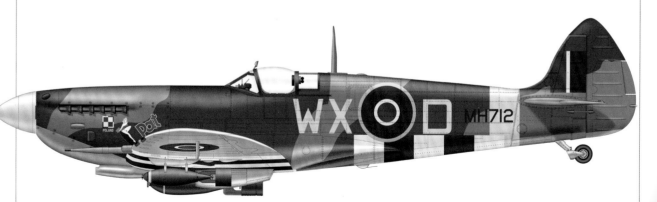

Supermarine Spitfire Mk.IX MH712. No 302 (Polish) Squadron. B.70 Deurne (Belgium), September 1944.
No 302 Sqn. was one of the last two Polish Spitfire-equipped units to switch to the Mk.IX in September 1943. It then entered the 2 TAF and took part in the D-Day landings. In February 1945, the unit received the Mk.XVI. In 18 months, the squadron only claimed one confirmed victory and two probable victories with the Mk.IX.

Supermarine Spitfire Mk.IX BS556. No 303 (Polish) Squadron. Northolt (United Kingdom), summer 1944.
No 303, another Polish squadron, received the Mk.IX in June 1943, but then transformed to the Mk.V in November, before going back to the Mk.IX in July 1944. It remained based in Great Britain until the end of the war, and was converted to Mustangs. The pilots of this squadron claimed twenty victories with the Mk.IX.

Supermarine Spitfire Mk.IX EN128. No 306 (Polish) Squadron. Northolt (United Kingdom), autumn 1942.
No 306 Sqn. was the first Polish fighter unit to receive the Mk.IX, which it did as early as September 1942, making the squadron one of the very first to use this type. But in spring 1943, after claiming approximately fifteen victories, the squadron reverted to the Mk.V. A year later, the squadron was equipped with Mustangs.

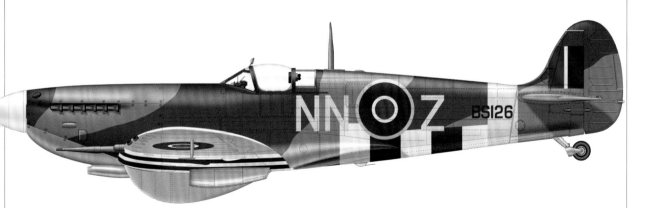

Supermarine Spitfire Mk.IX BS126. No 310 (Czechoslovak) Squadron. North Weald (United Kingdom), September 1944.
No 310 Sqn. took part in the D-Day landings with the Czechoslovak Wing, but, as it did not have a sufficient number of reserve pilots and expecting heavy losses, the Wing was removed from the 2 TAF and entered the ADBG after only two weeks of operations. The squadron's planes did not bare any distinctive markings, unlike the two other Czechoslovak fighter units.

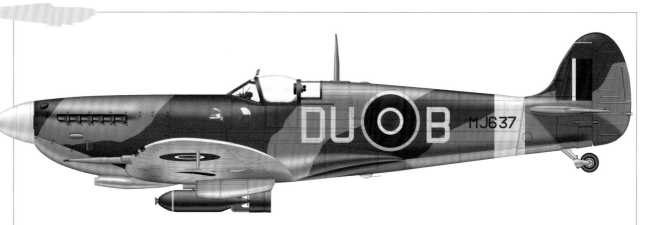

Supermarine Spitfire Mk.IX MJ637, W/O Frantisek Vravrinek. No 312 (Czechoslovak) Squadron. Mendlesham (United Kingdom), February 1944.
The three Czechoslovak fighter units were regrouped within No 134 Wing, which was part of the 2 TAF. No 312 followed in No 310's footsteps. W/O Vravrinek was one of the many pilots to have fled to Poland in 1939 and enrolled in the Polish Air Force. These pilots were subsequently interned in the Soviet Union when the latter invaded the country, and were freed in 1941 to be sent to Great Britain. The plane seen here bares the national Czechoslovak roundel which was present right from its formation, as well as the stork, the squadron's official insignia which drew its inspiration from the famous French "escadrille des Cigognes", as many of No 312 Sqn.'s first pilots had served in France in May and June 1940. This badge is often seen beginning with the Spitfire Mk.IX.

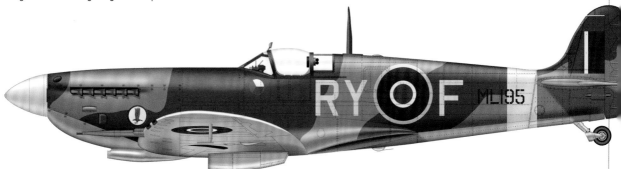

Supermarine Spitfire Mk.IX ML195. No 313 (Czechoslovak) Squadron. Manston (United Kingdom), spring 1945.
No 313 Sqn. was the last Czechoslovak fighter unit, just like No 310 and 312, to receive the Mk.IX in early 1944. The Mk.IX Spitfires of No 313 Sqn. also had the Czechoslovak roundel painted under the cockpit, whereas the squadron badge was placed on the underside of the engine cowling.

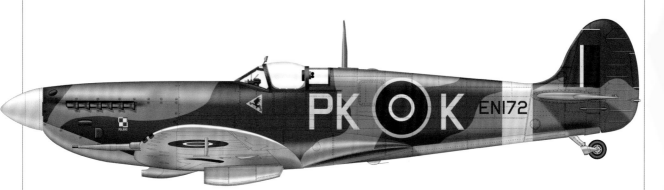

Supermarine Spitfire Mk.IX EN172, S/L Tadeusz Sawicz. No 315 (Polish) Squadron. Northolt (United Kingdom), spring 1943.
No 315 Sqn. received the Mk.IX in November 1942, but switched to the Mustang in March 1944. The squadron claimed half a dozen victories with the Mk.IX; in the first few months, the squadron was led by S/L Sawicz, who had seen action in Poland and where he shot down his first German planes.

Supermarine Spitfire Mk.IX EN527. S/L Marian Trzebinski. No 316 (Polish) Squadron. Northolt (United Kingdom), summer 1943.
No 316 (Polish) Sqn. only used the Mk.IX for six months, before going back to the Mk.V while they waited for the Mustangs. In the summer of 1943, the squadron claimed twenty kills. The squadron was then led by S/L Trzebinski, an experienced pilot who had seen action in Poland and France. The individual letter A was normally used by squadron leaders.

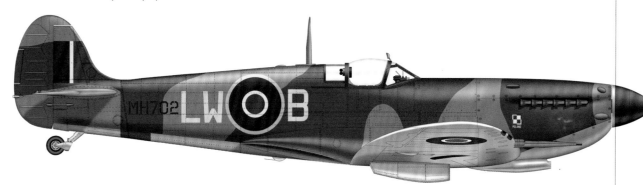

Supermarine Spitfire Mk.IX MH702. No 318 (Polish) Squadron. Forli (Italy), spring 1945.
In March 1943, No 318 Sqn. was the last squadron of the Polish Air Force to be formed; it was a tactical reconnaissance unit and also the only Polish squadron to be deployed in Italy, where it was under the command of the British 8th Army. It initially flew with Hurricanes, but began to use the Spitfire Mk.V in March 1944, and afterwards the Mk.IX in November of the same year.

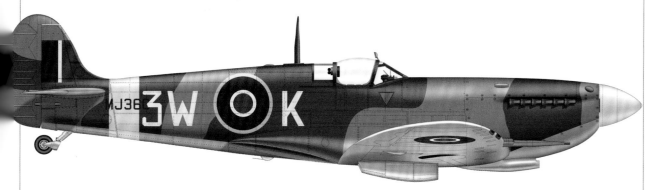

Supermarine Spitfire Mk.IX MJ360. No 322 (Dutch) Squadron. Fairwood Common (United Kingdom), autumn 1944.
After having shown its talent for shooting down V1 flying bombs with its Griffon-engined Spitfires in the summer of 1944, No 322 moved over to the Mk.IX in order to take part in ground-attack missions in its home country of the Netherlands. It used this type for four months before receiving the Mk.XVI.

53

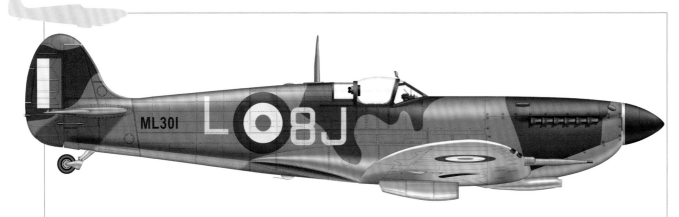

Supermarine Spitfire Mk.IX ML301. No 326 (French) Squadron. Stuttgart (Germany), autumn 1944.
No 326 Sqn. was the British name for the French GC 2/7 "Nice" squadron; it used Spitfires as soon as it joined the RAF. In April 1944, it was mostly using the Mk.IX when it was fighting in Italy and southern France. The squadron was sent to Germany in early 1945. From autumn 1944 onwards, the Spitfires it used were systematically painted with French colours. MJ345 was one of the planes that were ceded to France at the end of the war. No 326 Sqn. had officially been given the 8J code, but the code only started to be regularly used in the last weeks of the war; the squadron had been using a single letter until that point in time. The squadron claimed fifteen victories with the Mk.IX.

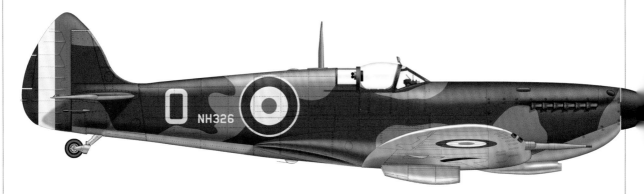

Supermarine Spitfire Mk.IX NH326. No 328 (French) Squadron. Dijon (France), early 1945.
No 328 Sqn. was actually the GC 1/7 "Provence" unit of the Armée de l'Air, which had joined the RAF. In late 1944, the unit was based in France in order to support the French troops. The French markings started to be regularly used in the second half of 1944.

Supermarine Spitfire Mk.IX MK305. No 329 (French) Squadron. Perranporth (United Kingdom), March 1944.
No 329 Sqn. ("Cigognes") was created in Great Britain in early 1944 with Armée de l'Air staff who had been based in North Africa. After a brief time with the Mk.V, the squadron took the Mk.IX on charge and mostly used this mark for ground-attack missions with the 2 TAF before its transfer to the Armée de l'Air in November 1945. MK305 was one of the first Mk.IX to be taken on charge; the plane was lost in an accident in May 1944. At that time, the planes of this squadron did not bear any distinctive markings, whereas in the last months of the war, the famous "Escadrille des Cigognes" insignia was painted beneath the cockpit.

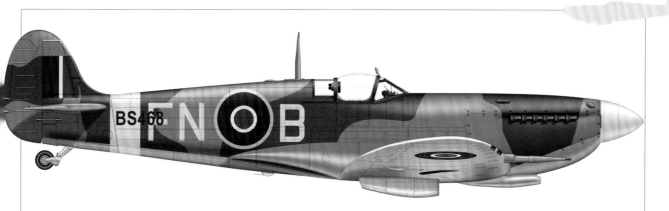

Supermarine Spitfire Mk.IX BS468. No 331 (Norwegian) Squadron. North Weald (United Kingdom), autumn 1942.
No 331 Sqn. (Norwegian) was one of the first RAF units to put the Mk.IX to use. BS468 was delivered to the RAF on 25 September and then to No 331 Sqn. the next day. The squadron kept its Mk.IX until its transfer to the Norwegian Air Force in November 1945. In two and half years of flying with the Mk.IX, the squadron became one of the best Mk.IX-equipped squadrons with 120 kills.

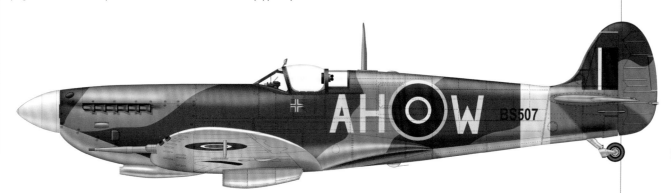

Supermarine Spitfire Mk.IX BS507. No 332 (Norwegian) Squadron. North Weald (United Kingdom), autumn 1942.
No 332 Sqn. received the Mk.IX shortly after No 331 Sqn.; the two units followed the same path until November 1945. However, No 332 was less successful as it only claimed fifty victories with the Mk.IX. It is worth noting the Norwegian pennant, which was not often painted on the Mk.IX.

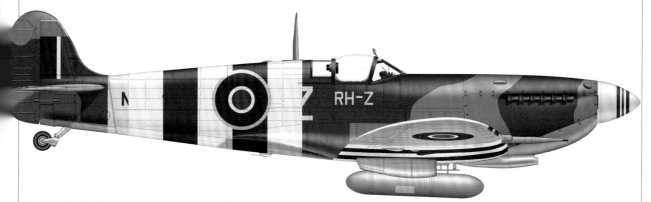

Supermarine Spitfire Mk.IX NH171. No 332 (Norwegian) Squadron. Bognor (United Kingdom), June 1944.
In 1944, the Norwegians replaced the little pennant painted under the cockpit with their national markings, which were more visible, and opted to paint the propeller cone with Norwegian colours, which made them more recognisable in flight. NH171 seen here is painted with invasion stripes, but, unlike the other units, the mechanics painted over the code letters, which had to be repainted under the cockpit in a somewhat usual shape.

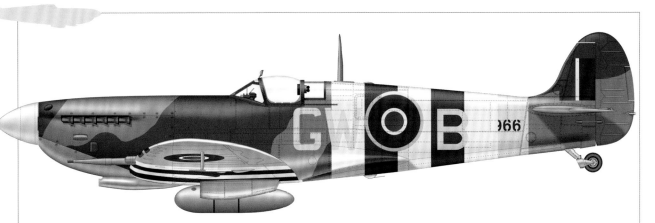

Supermarine Spitfire Mk.IX MJ966. No 340 (Free French) Squadron. Merston (United Kingdom), June 1944.
No 340 Sqn. briefly used the Mk.IX between October 1942 and March 1943 and between January 1944 and February 1945. During these two periods, they claimed thirty victories. MJ966 seen here is not painted with the usual Croix de Lorraine, because the ground crews, with the rapid rotation of the aircraft and the great number of daily missions in June 1944, did not always have the time to paint the planes completely.

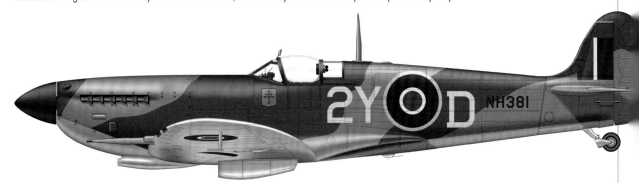

Supermarine Spitfire Mk.IX NH381. No 345 (French) Squadron. B.85/Schjindel (Netherlands), March 1945.
Formed in February 1944 with personnel of the Armée de l'Air d'Afrique du Nord, No 345 Sqn. (GC II/2 "Berry") only switched to the Mk.IX in September; it retained this type until April 1945, when it received the Mk.XVI.

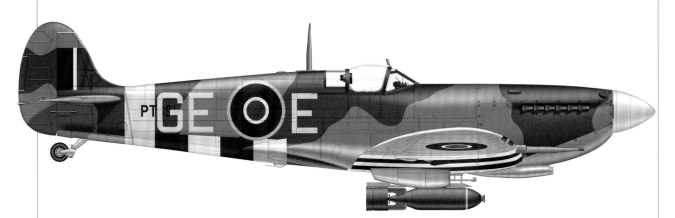

Supermarine Spitfire Mk.IX PT891. No 349 (Belgian) Squadron. B.53/Merville (France), October 1944.
In February 1944, No 349 Sqn. swapped its Mk.V for the Mk.IX. From then until May 1945, the unit was almost permanently engaged in support missions for the 2 TAF. Even though it specialised in ground troops support missions, the squadron managed to claim five victories.

Supermarine Spitfire Mk.IX ML137. No 350 (Belgian) Squadron. Westhampnett (United Kingdom), summer 1944.
None of No 350 Sqn.'s sixty victories, the first Belgian unit to be created on British soil, were claimed using the Mk.IX. This mark was indeed only used for a few weeks, between December 1943 and March 1944 and between July and August 1944. The squadron established most of its reputation with the Mk.XIV.

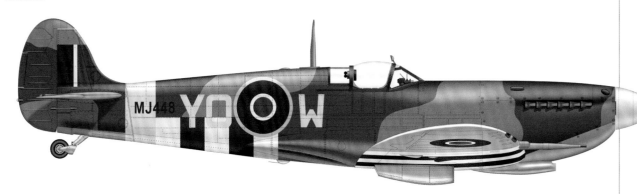

Supermarine Spitfire Mk.IX MJ448. S/L Roderick I. A. Smith (RCAF). No 401 (RCAF) Squadron. B.68/Le Culot (France), autumn 1944.
No 401 (Canadian) Sqn. claimed forty victories with the Spitfire Mk.IX, including one against a Me 262 and three against the Ar 234, which makes it one of the best Mk.IX-equipped units; it started receiving this mark in July 1942. In October 1944, the squadron was led by S/L Rod Smith, a Battle of Malta veteran, who had 14 confirmed victories (one of which was shared) to his name.

Supermarine Spitfire Mk.IX BS152. P/O Lorne M. Cameron (RCAF). No 402 (RCAF) Squadron. Kenley (United Kingdom), September 1942.
No 402 (Canadian) Sqn. only used the Mk.IX for a short time, between August 1942 and March 1943 and in July and August 1944. Only half a dozen victories were claimed using this version, one of which by P/O Cameron on 27 February 1943, the first of his five confirmed victories. It is worth noting the "RCAF Overseas" roundel, which was starting to appear at this time, as well as the personal insignia that does not in any way conform to regulations!

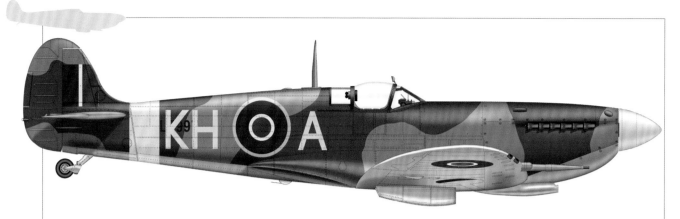

Supermarine Spitfire Mk.IX LZ997, F/L Walter A. G. Conrad (RCAF). No 403 (RCAF) Squadron. Kenley (United Kingdom), summer 1943.
The Canadian pilots of No 403 Sqn., which started using the Mk.IX in January 1943, claimed more than 90 victories, two of which were by "Wally" Conrad, who had claimed eight victories in the Middle East, three of which were shared. He scored one kill with LZ997 on 6 July 1943. No 403 Sqn. changed over to the Mk.XVI in December 1944.

Supermarine Spitfire Mk.IX MH850. F/L George W. Johnson (RCAF). No 411 (RCAF) Squadron, Tangmere (United Kingdom), spring 1944.
George Johnson is another Canadian pilot with 8 victories to his name, all of which were claimed with the Mk.IX, even though, by spring 1944, he was yet to claim a single kill. No 411 Sqn. started using the Mk.IX in October 1943 and claimed more than 70 victories up to May 1945, two of which were against Me 262s and two against Mistels.

Supermarine Spitfire Mk.IX MH883. F/L George F. Beurling (RCAF). No 412 (RCAF) Squadron. Biggin Hill (United Kingdom), early 1944.
"Buzz" Beurling was a Canadian ace whose last operational posting was with No 412 Sqn. This squadron had been equipped with the Mk.IX since November 1943. Beurling claimed one of the squadron's first victories with the Mk.IX on 30 December 1943; this victory was also to be his last before he returned to Canada. Concerning the squadron as a whole, it claimed a hundred victories up to May 1945.

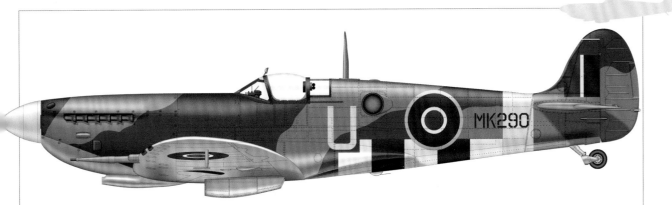

Supermarine Spitfire FR.IX MK290. No 414 (RCAF) Squadron. B.78/Eindhoven (Netherlands), autumn 1944.
The Spitfire Mk.IX reconnaissance types were mostly used in the Mediterranean, because in Europe, this kind of mission was conferred more to the Allison-engined Mustang which was originally used by No 414 Sqn. However, as this model became rare in 1944, the squadron, integrated into the 2 TAF, had to be entirely re-equipped with the FR.IX in August 1944 before receiving the Spitfire FR.XIV in April 1945. Despite the role attributed to No 414 Sqn., its reconnaissance Mk.IXs shot down half a dozen German planes.

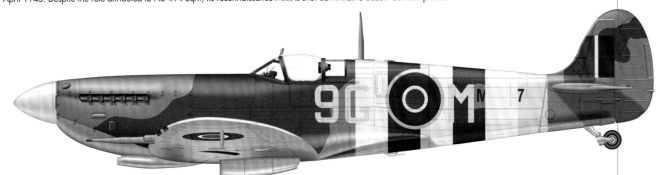

Supermarine Spitfire LF.IXB MK417. F/O Bruce M. McKenzie. No 441 (RCAF) Squadron, Ford (United Kingdom), June 1944.
No 441 Sqn. was an RCAF unit sent to Europe in early 1944 with the D-Day landings in mind, whose original name (No 125 Sqn.) was changed to No 441 Sqn. It was part of the 2 TAF before joining Fighter Command in autumn 1944. It claimed 49 confirmed or probable victories in one year of combat. Bruce McKenzie was one of the squadron's pilots who claimed some of these victories by shooting down an Fw 190 with MK417 on 13 July 1944.

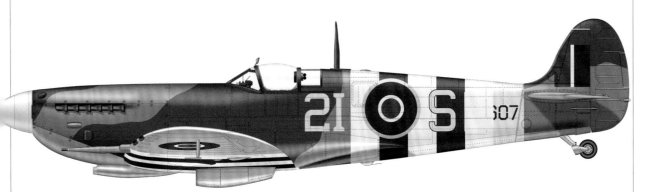

Supermarine Spitfire LF.IX MK607. F/O Luis Perez-Gomez (Mexico). No 443 (RCAF) Squadron. B.3/St-Croix (France), June 1944.
No 443 Sqn. was formed in February 1944 with personnel from No 127 Sqn. RCAF. Among its pilots was Luis Perez-Gomez, a Mexican who enlisted in the Canadian Air Force; he was killed in a dogfight against some Fw 190 on 16 June 1944, becoming the only Mexican pilot to be killed in action in Europe during the Second World War.
No 443 Sqn. kept its Mk.IXs until January 1945, when it switched to Mk.XVI. This unit was led in June 1944 by S/L Harry McLeod, who had more than twenty victories to his name.

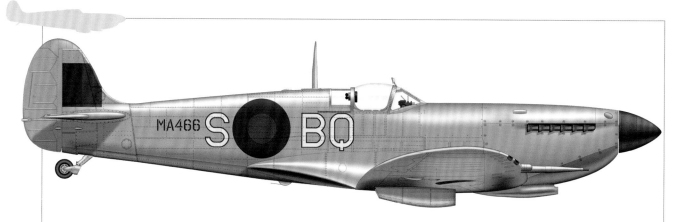

Supermarine Spitfire Mk.IX MA466. No 451 (RAAF) Squadron. Poretta (Corsica, France), spring 1944.
When No 451 Sqn. became a fighter unit, it received the Spitfire Mk.V, which were to be soon replaced by the Mk.IX. In spring 1944, the unit was stationed in Corsica, from where it took part in escort missions. The first Mk.IXs it took on charge had been given the camouflage scheme reserved for high altitude planes. In November, this squadron left Corsica to join the 2 TAF, and was equipped with the Mk.XVI after having claimed a dozen victories with the Mk.IX.

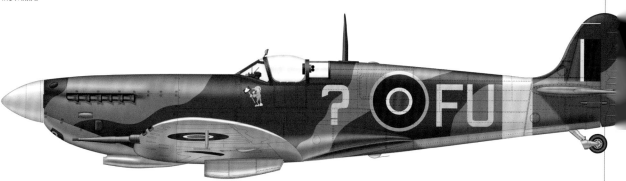

Supermarine Spitfire Mk.IX BS224, F/L Donald G. Andrews (RAAF). No 453 (RAAF) Squadron. Hornchurch (United Kingdom), spring 1943.
In 1943 and 1944, No 453 Sqn. was the only Australian fighter unit present on British soil. Before receiving the Mk.XVI, it claimed thirty victories with the Mk.IX. The question mark was borne by a few planes belonging to No 453 Sqn. Andrews kept his personal insignia when he was leading No 453 Sqn. and the Coltishall Wing.

Supermarine Spitfire Mk.IX ML407, F/O John A. Houlton (RNZAF). No 485 (NZ) Squadron. Selsey (United Kingdom), June 1944.
No 485 Sqn. was the only New Zealand fighter unit to use Spitfire (which they started flying in 1941). The squadron received the Mk.IX in February 1944. It was then incorporated into the 2 TAF, which it followed into Germany, claiming forty victories on the way. Among the squadron's victorious pilots was "Johnnie" Houlton, the New Zealand ace and Malta veteran, who shot down a Bf 109 whilst flying ML407 on 12 June 1944. Houlton survived the war. It is worth noting the letter V placed in front of the squadron code ("OU").

Supermarine Spitfire Mk. IX MA817. No 501 (County of Gloucester) Squadron. Friston (United Kingdom), spring 1944.
No 501 Sqn. was one of the Spitfire units that used the Mk.V the longest; in June 1943, it received a few Mk.IX to add to its Mk.V. The Mk.IX bore numbers, and not letters, a situation that was set straight in spring 1944. No more than a dozen Mk.IX bore the 501 code. The squadron transformed to the Tempest Mk.V shortly after.

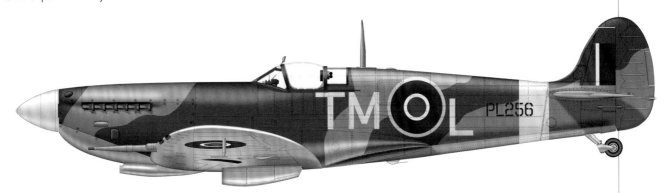

Supermarine Spitfire Mk.IX PL256, S/L George C. Banning-Lover. No 504 (County of Nottingham) Squadron. Manston (United Kingdom), autumn 1944.
When, in January 1944, No 504 Sqn. left Scotland for southern England, it swapped its Mk.Vs for the Mk.IX. But the squadron's beginnings with this mark proved to be dramatic as eight of the squadron's planes were destroyed on the ground during a raid on 23 February 1944. After that, the squadron was on the offensive, but remained based in Great Britain until the end of the war, claiming only one victory on 22 April 1944.

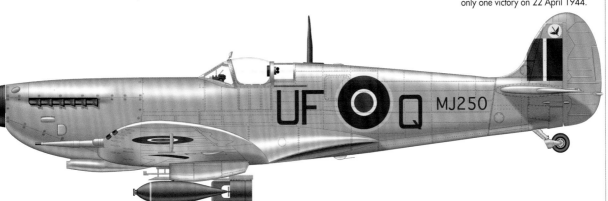

Supermarine Spitfire Mk.IX MJ250. F/L Desmond Ibbotson. No 601 (County of London) Squadron. Perugia (Italy), summer 1944.
Desmond Ibboston, a British ace who served in North Africa (mainly with No 601 Sqn.) finished his second tour of operations in July 1944, when No 601 Sqn. received the Mk.IX as a replacement for its Mk.VIII. He chose MJ250, which was one of the first Spitfires not to be camouflaged. The reason why this factory-painted model had its camouflage scheme removed remains unknown, but this particularity is surely what made Ibbotson choose it, in order to distinguish himself from the others. The squadron insignia painted on the tail fin was a common practice within No 601 Sqn. in 1944.

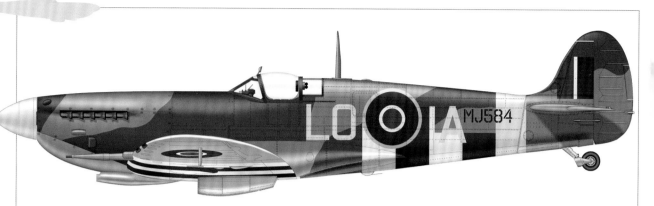

Supermarine Spitfire Mk.IX MJ584. No 602 (City of Glasgow) Squadron. B.11/Longues (France), summer 1944.
Starting in September 1943, No 602 Sqn. used the Mk.IX almost uninterruptedly, before changing over to the Mk.XVI in November 1944. During this period, the squadron claimed forty victories, 25 of which were post D-Day.

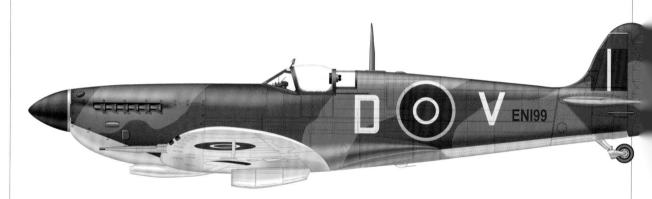

Supermarine Spitfire Mk.IX EN199, No 1435 Squadron, Grottaglie (Italy), autumn 1944.
No 1435 Sqn. was an anomaly in the British system, as its name does not follow the standard numbering and corresponds to a section normally reserved for the Flights. In fact, the unit was originally a Flight based in Malta, but that quickly grew to the size of a squadron, and claimed many victories against the Axis forces. This unusual designation was officialised afterwards. During its entire existence, this unit bore the letter V as a code, even when it was based in Italy, where two-letter squadron codes had become compulsory.

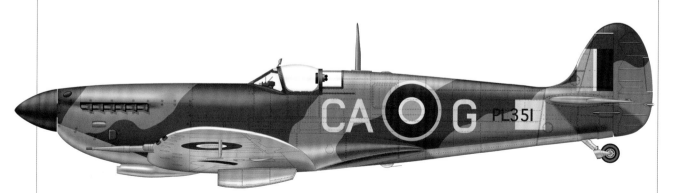

Supermarine Spitfire Mk.IX PL351. Major Cecil A. Golding. No 3 Squadron SAAF. Pontedera (Italy), early 1945.
No 3 Sqn. of the SAAF received the "CA" code in the autumn of 1944. When Major Golding took command in December 1944, he logically chose the individual letter G for his personal plane; the plane's complete code (CA°G) corresponded to his initials. It is worth noting the partly worn fuselage band, as well as the standard SAAF roundel with the orange centre, which was systematically used in South-African squadrons.

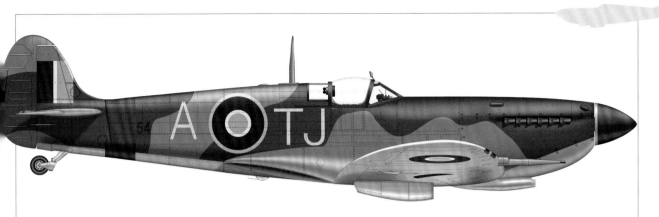

Supermarine Spitfire Mk.IX JL254. No 7 Squadron SAAF. Grotaglie (Italy), autumn 1944.
No 7 Sqn., another South-African unit equipped with the Spitfire Mk.IX, started fighting in Italy in April 1944. In addition to the identification letters, this unit had also chosen a red fuselage band.

Supermarine Spitfire Mk.IX MH705. No 10 Squadron SAAF. Idku (Egypt), summer 1944.
No 10 Sqn. SAAF had a short career, spanning from May to October 1944, and was equipped with both the Spitfire MK.V and Mk.IX, the latter being reserved for high-altitude sorties. This unit, which was limited in Egypt to aerial defence missions, was disbanded due to the lack of any threat and activity. It is worth noting that this unit did not have squadron identification letters, but had a red and sky-coloured propeller cone as its distinctive marking.

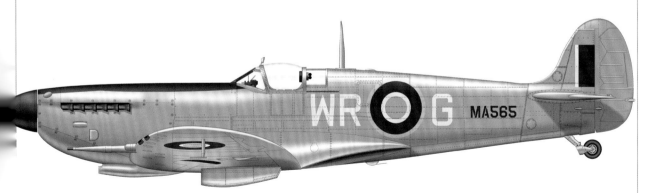

Supermarine Spitfire Mk.IX MA565. No 40 Squadron SAAF. San Angelo (Italy), spring 1944.
No 40 Sqn. SAAF, a tactical reconnaissance unit, was equipped with the Mk.IX as early as June 1943. Even though most of the planes had a standard camouflage scheme, some were given a grey-based camouflage scheme (here, probably a Medium Sea Grey) in order to be less visible for certain missions, even though the effect is somewhat diminished by the SAAF roundels. The antireflection panel was inspired by USAAF planes.

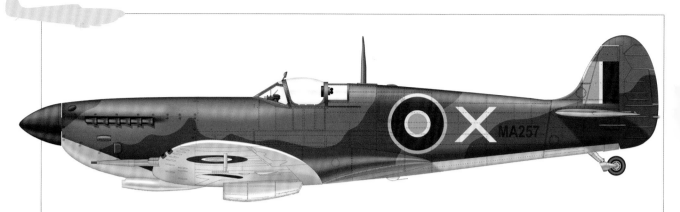

Supermarine Spitfire Mk.IX MA257. No 41 Squadron SAAF. Lakatamia (Cyprus), autumn 1944.
No 41 Sqn., a South African tactical reconnaissance unit, became a fighter unit during the war. It claimed two confirmed victories, one of which was against a Ju 88 on 24 April 1944. MA257 was one of the two victorious planes, which explains the presence of the swastika.

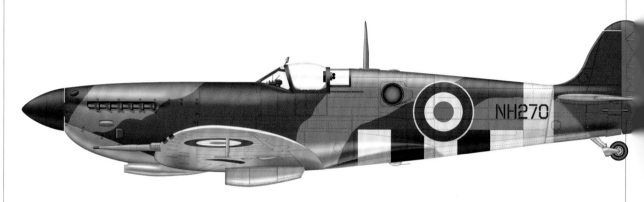

Supermarine Spitfire Mk.IX NH270. GR II/33 "Savoie". Luxeuil (France), late 1944.
"The 33 unit", a squadron famous for the F-5 Lightnings belonging to the I/33 "Belfort" squadron, had a second, lesser-known squadron, the 2/33, which flew Spitfires in 1943-44, with the Mk.IX arriving in the second half of 1944. In 1945, the F-6 Mustang replaced the Spitfire for reconnaissance missions.

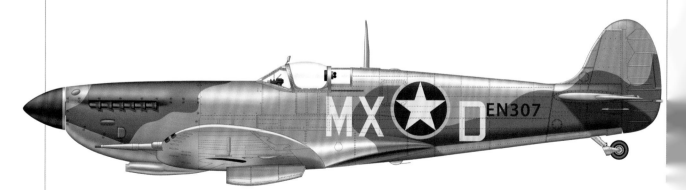

Supermarine Spitfire Mk.IX EN307. 307th FS/31st FG. Thelepte (Tunisia), March 1943.
The Americans were among the first to put the Mk.IX to use in the Mediterranean and towards the end of 1943, the model was generalised among the 31st FG (except for the 308th FS which used the Mk.VIII). EN307 seen here was not returned to the RAF as it was destroyed in Italy on 15 December 1943.

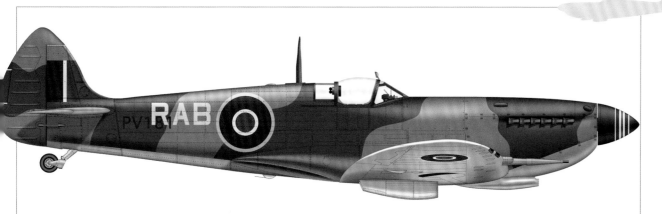

Supermarine Spitfire Mk.IX PV181, W/C Rolfe A. Berg. No 132 Wing. B.79/Woensdrecht (Netherlands), January 1945.
Rolfe Berg was a Norwegian ace who served with No 331 (Norwegian) Sqn. from 1942 onwards, and with six confirmed victories to his name. In 1945, he led No 132 Wing, which was made up of, among others, two other Norwegian fighter units (No 331 and 332 Sqns.). W/C Berg was shot down and killed by flak on 3 February whilst flying the plane seen here, which bore, as per tradition, the initials of the pilots surname and first name. It is worth noting that PV181 conformed at the time to the regulations introduced in early January 1945 within the 2 TAF, with the lower surface roundels with the yellow circle. The Norwegian national colours painted on the propeller cone are the only distinctive marking.

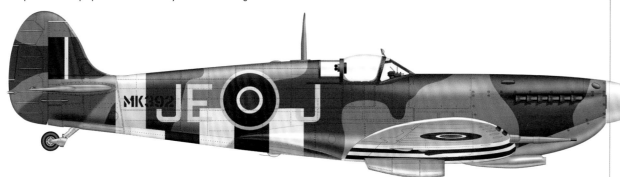

Supermarine Spitfire Mk.IX MK392, W/C James E. Johnson. No 127 Wing, B.2/Bazenville (France), July 1944.
"Johnny" Johnson, the greatest of British aces, led 127 Wing during the D-Day landings. During the Battle of Normandy, he claimed ten confirmed victories, including three doubles, all but one with the MK392 seen here.

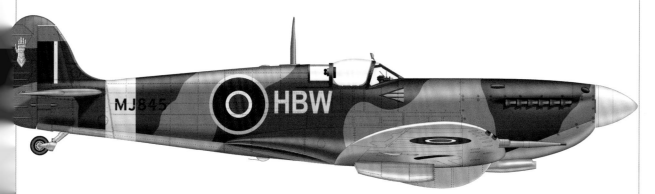

Supermarine Spitfire Mk.IX MJ845. W/C Harold Bird-Wilson. No 122 Airfield, Gravesend (United Kingdom), late 1943.
Harold Bird-Wilson was an RAF ace who had seen action in the Battles of France and Britain in 1940 with No 17 Sqn. In 1943, he was WingCo flying of 122 Airfield, which included Nos 19, 65 and 122 Squadrons, which were using the Spitfire Mk.IX before transferring to Mustang. Bird-Wilson retired from the RAF in 1974 as an Air-Vice Marshal. It is worth noting the gloved hand on the fin which was a reminder of his time with No 17 Sqn., as well as the Wing Commander's pennant.

Supermarine Spitfire Mk.IX MK483. W/C Tomas Vybiral. No 134 (Czecoslovak) Wing. Appledram (United Kingdom), June 1944.
The three Czechoslovak squadrons briefly took part in the first phases of the Normandy landings. At that time it was led by Tomas Vybiral's who had fled his country before the war, when the Germans invaded. He then fought alongside the French with a Curtiss plane in May-June 1940. Vybiral survived the war, but had to leave his homeland once again after the Prague coup in 1948. He chose the first two letters of his name as a code, which is rather unusual for a Wing Commander.

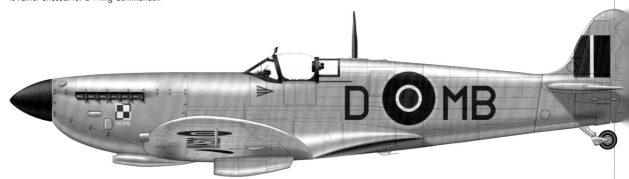

Supermarine Spitfire Mk.IX MK520. W/C Marian Duryasz. Germany, June 1945.
Marion Duryasz was a Polish pilot who managed to flee to Great Britain in early 1940. He took part in the Battle of Britain with No 213 Sqn., flying a Hurricane, and then served in various Polish squadrons (Nos 302, 308 and 317). His last operational post was as commander of No 302 Sqn. between June 1944 and January 1945. In January 1945, he was transferred to the Polish headquarters of the 2 TAF. He returned to Poland after the war and served with the Polish Air Force. It is worth noting the serial number under the wings, which had been reintroduced in 1945, the removed guns, and the Polish and Wing Commander badges.

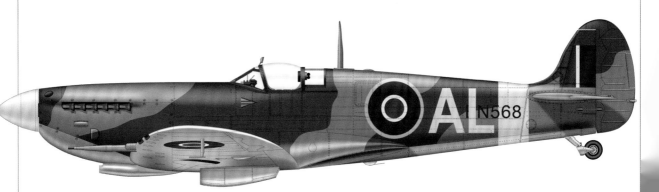

Supermarine Spitfire Mk.IX EN568. W/C Alan C. Deere (NZ). Biggin Hill (United Kingdom), summer 1943.
Serving in the RAF, New-Zealander Al Deere became one of No 54 Sqn.'s best-known pilots in 1940. In 1943, he became the leader of the Biggin Hill Wing, and claimed his last victories with the plane seen here on 14 July 1943. It is worth noting that he chose the two letters of his nickname "Al" as an identification code.

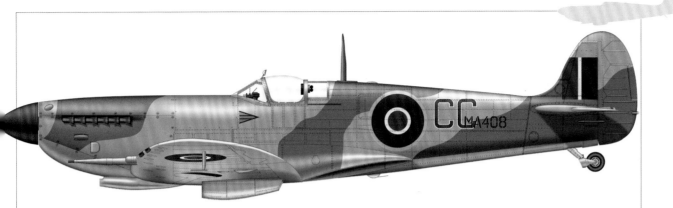

Supermarine Spitfire Mk.IX MA408. W/C Colin F. Gray (NZ). 322 Wing, Lentini (Sicily), summer 1943.
Colin Gray, another New-Zealander in the RAF, was in No 54 with Al Deere, and claimed his first victories in May 1940. Meanwhile, in 1942, he chose to serve overseas, and was subsequently sent to North Africa in 1943, where, in the middle of the same year, he was promoted to leader of the 322 Wing. Gray ended the war with 29 confirmed victories, two of which were shared, thus becoming the first New Zealand ace of the Second World War.

Supermarine Spitfire Mk.IX MH944. Colonel Daniel W. Human (SAAF). 7 Wing (SAAF). Italy, winter 1944-45.
"Johnny" Human was a South African ace who fought in the desert in 1942-43. In early 1945, he was the leader of SAAF 7th Fighter Wing. His code was made up of letters of his nickname and his surname. It is worth noting the unusual placing of the wing commander pennant.

Supermarine Spitfire Mk.IX EN329. Colonel Fred M. Dean. 31st FG USAAF. North Africa, early 1943.
When the 31st FG arrived in North Africa in late 1942, the unit was led by Colonel Dean. In early 1943, the Americans took their first Mk.IX on charge, and Dean chose EN329 as his personal plane, on which he had his initials painted, obviously inspired by the privileges enjoyed by the RAF. It is worth noting the serial number painted on the top of the tail fin.

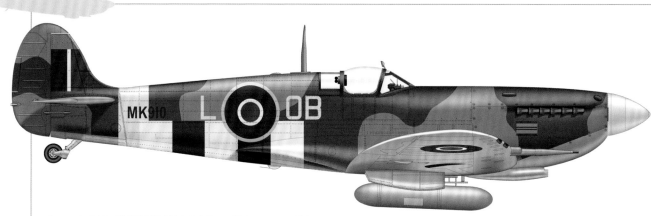

Supermarine Spitfire Mk.IX MK910. AVM Leslie O. Brown. 84 Group, summer 1944.
Air Vice Marshall Brown, a Great War veteran of South-African origin, served among various headquarters in the Middle East before taking the command of 84 Group of the 2 TAF in November 1943. His plane bore the distinctive markings of his rank, including his initials. Meanwhile, in order to avoid confusion between a plane of No 602 Sqn. (coded "LO") and his, he chose to move his initials.

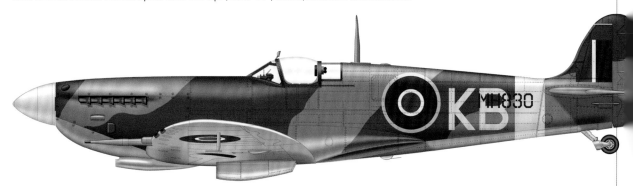

Supermarine Spitfire Mk.IX MH830. W/C Kaj Birksted (Denmark). No 132 (Norwegian) Wing. North Weald, January 1944.
Kaj Birksted was a Danish pilot who managed to flee to Sweden when his country was invaded by the Germans in April 1940. He first went to Norway, but then made his way to Great Britain, where he enrolled in the RAF, becoming one of the rare Danes within this institution. He joined Norwegian No 331 Sqn. in 1941, claiming his first victories there. He became the squadron's commander in September 1942. For his second tour of operations, he was named as commander of 132 Norwegian Wing and claimed his last victory Wing Commander on 23 January 1944 whilst flying his plane ("MH830/KB"). His tally of kills reached a total of eleven victories, including one shared. Birksted finished the war as commander of a Mustang Wing.

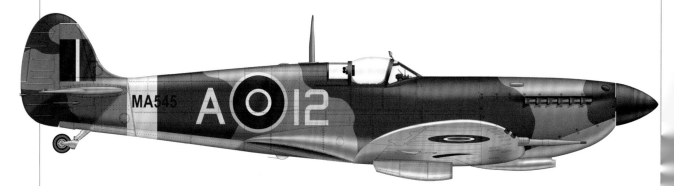

Supermarine Spitfire Mk.IX MA545. 5 RFU. Sinello (Italy), winter 1944-45.
The 5 Refresher Flying Unit's role was to provide flying experience to pilots on operational planes used by the Desert Air Force. In late 1944, having many different types of fighter planes, it had 25 Spitfire Mk.IX, including the MA545.

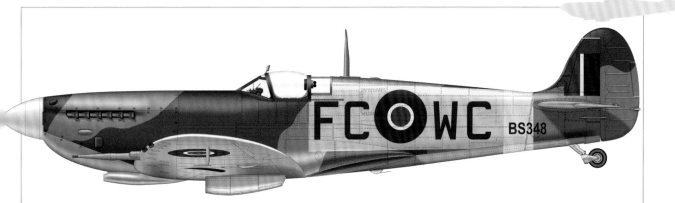

Supermarine Spitfire Mk.IX BS348. EFS. Hullavington, 1946.
The Empire Flying School was a unit that trained flying instructors and that used a great variety of planes in 1945, one of which was BS348, one of the very first Mk.IX transformed from a Mk.V in 1942. The codes of this unit went from FCT to FCX. It is worth noting the colour yellow, which was reserved for training planes.

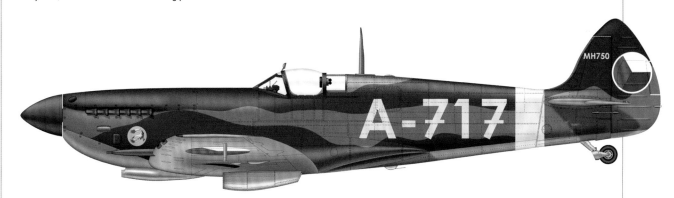

Supermarine Spitfire Mk.IX A-717. Letecke Vojenske Akademie (LVA). Hradec Kralove (Czechoslovakia), late 1940s.
The three former RAF fighter units that were made up of Czech pilots (Nos 310, 312 and 313 Sqns.) turned out to be the main structure of the 1., 2., and 3. LD (Letecka Divize) respectively, as well as certain second line units such as the air force academy. The A-717 seen here has retained the 2.LD/312 Sqn. insignia. The Spitfires kept their serial numbers nonetheless, and the latter were often painted on the tail fin, as seen here. MH750 was later sold to Israel.

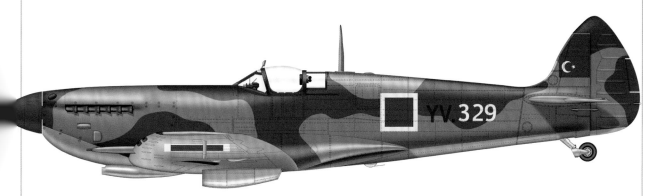

Supermarine Spitfire Mk.IX 6329. 5th air regiment of the Türk Hava Kuvvetleri (Turkish Air Force). Bursa (Turkey), late 1940s.
Already a Mk.V user, Turkey wanted to modernise its Air Force after the war; it purchased almost 200 Mk.IX, all but a few with clipped wings, that were delivered in 1947 and 1948. In total, 168 were put into service: they received the Turkish numbers from 6201 to 6369. They were taken out of service in 1954.

69

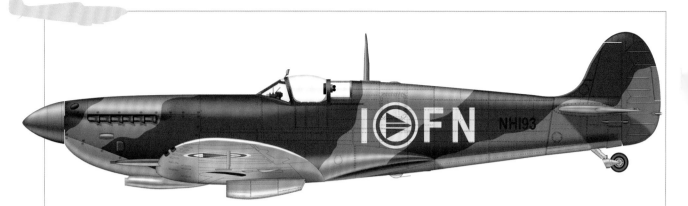

Supermarine Spitfire Mk.IX NH193. Skvadron 331. Kjevik (Norway), 1951.
After having used Spitfires during the war, the two Norwegian squadrons returned to their homeland in 1945, and the Mk.IX became the standard fighter plane for the Kongelige Norske Luftforsvaret until the arrival of the first jets in the 1950s. Norway used 71 Mk.IXs in total.

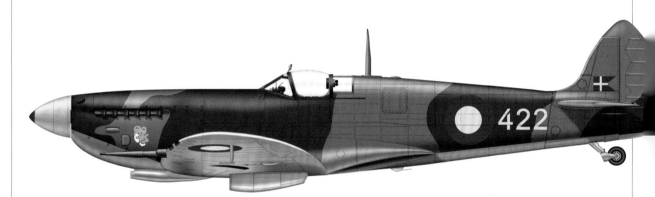

Supermarine Spitfire Mk.IX 41-422. 725 Eskadrille. Karup (Denmark), 1951.
Denmark put 45 Spitfire Mk.IXs into service, 38 of which bore the numbers 41-401 to 436 (two of them were not given a number). They were delivered in 1947 and used until 1955. All of them were of the HF version, and were adapted for high altitude interception.

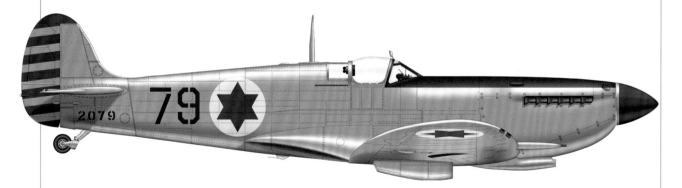

Supermarine Spitfire Mk.IX 2079. Tayeset 107 of the Heyl Ha' Avir. Ramat David (Israel), early 1950s.
Israel purchased one hundred Spitfire Mk.IXs at the state's creation in 1948. Most of them were sold by Czechoslovakia. Ninety were put into service, receiving numbers 2001 to 2090; they were used in the early fighting against the Arabs, and were retired from service in 1956.

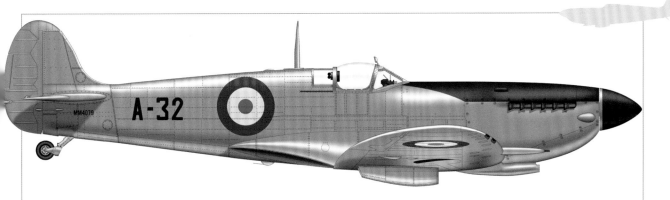

Supermarine Spitfire Mk.IX MM.4079. RVSM of the AMI (Aviazione Militare Italiana). Roma-Centocelle (Italy), late 1940s.
Great Britain sold 145 Spitfire Mk.IX to Italy between 1946 and 1947. These planes were stored in Italy (where they were given the matricola militare (MM) from MM4000 to MM413, MM4284 and MM4286). In addition to that were two Mk.IX sold by Turkey in 1949 (MM4286 and 4287). They were put into service until 1952, equipping two fighter squadrons as well as second line units such as the Reparto Volo Stato Maggiore, a squadron set up in order to allow staff officers their monthly flight time quota.

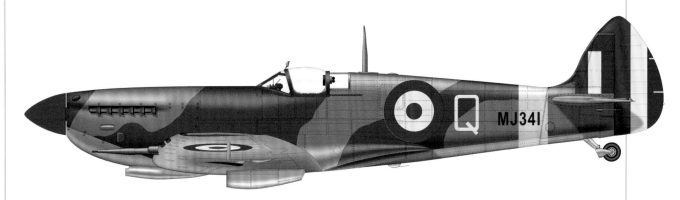

Supermarine Spitfire Mk.IX MJ341. GC 2/4 "La Fayette" of the French Armée de l'Air. Hanoi (Indochina), 1947.
France was an important Spitfire user during and after the war. In total, 359 Spitfire Mk.IX were taken on charge by the French, most of which after the war. The Spitfire was the fighter plane they used in the early phases of the conflicts in Indochina. France used them until 1953.

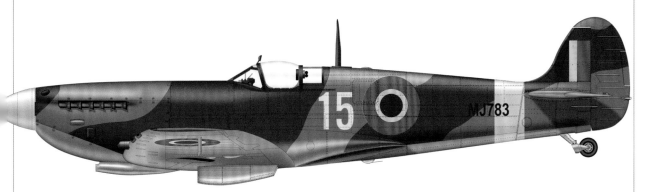

Supermarine Spitfire Mk.IX SM15. Belgian air force advanced flying school (FAéB). Brustem (Belgium), 1948.
Belgium was a traditional customer of the British war industry, so it seemed natural for the country to look towards Britain when it wanted to rebuild its air force. The Spitfire XIV was chosen as the main fighter plane, but 43 Spitfire Mk.IX (from SM1 to SM43) were taken on charge nonetheless for secondary missions, such as advanced fighter training. It is worth noting the mix of RAF (MJ783) and Belgian numbers (15 for the SM15).

Supermarine Spitfire Mk.IX SM39. Belgian air force advanced flying school (FAéB). Brustem (Belgium), 1953.
The Belgian Spitfire Mk.IXs retained their original British camouflage scheme until the 1950s, when the scheme was gradually replaced with a more sober pattern. It is worth noting the yellow stripes, a colour inspired by the RAF.

Supermarine Spitfire Mk.IX H-68. No 322 Sqn. of the Koninklijke Luchtmacht (KLu, Dutch Air Force). Semarang (Java), 1948.
In order to repress the insurrection, the Netherlands sent No 332 Sqn. along with 20 Spitfires to Indonesia, with numbers H-50 to H-69 after 1949. The surviving planes were brought back to the Netherlands once Indonesia obtained independence. These Spitfires had been repainted with a mix of probably Australian paint, with upper surfaces of a colour close to Foliage Green.

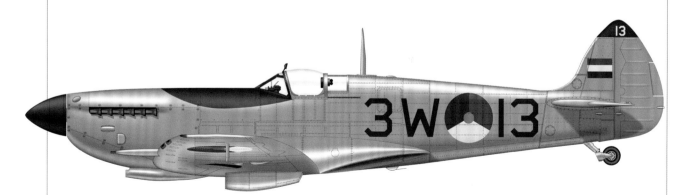

Supermarine Spitfire Mk.IX H-13. No, 322 Sqn. of the KLu. Twente (Netherlands), 1951.
The Dutch, just like the Belgians, chose the Spitfire Mk.IX for fighter training after the war, and purchased 35 of them (serial numbers H-1 to H-35). When No 322 Sqn. returned to the Netherlands, it had to go back to flying the Spitfire Mk.IX, borrowed from the fighter school (Jachtvlieggschool) while they waited to be converted to the Gloster Meteor.

Supermarine Spitfire Mk.IX H-97 of the Jachtvlieggschool of the KLu. Twente (Netherlands), 1949.
Holland was among the rare countries to have used the two-seater Spitfires, as they took 3 of them on charge in 1948 (H-97 to H-99). They were used by the advanced fighter training school. Two were lost in accidents.

Supermarine Spitfire T.IX 158. (A) Flying Training School of the Irish Air Corps (IAC). Baldonnel (Ireland), late 1950s.
Ireland bought, in addition to reconditioned Seafires, six two-seater Spitfires that were taken on charge in June and July 1951 (numbers 158 to 163); they remained in service until 1961.

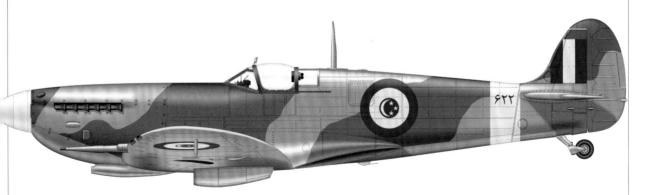

Supermarine Spitfire Mk.IX 622. No 2 Sqn. of the REAF (Royal Egyptian Air Force). Almaza (Egypt), 1948.
Egypt used 40 Mk.IX in total (including one two-seater) to equip two fighter units, No 1 and No 2 Sqns. These planes were engaged in the first Israelo-Arab war, where they fought the Israeli Spitfires. Many were lost in action at this time.

SPITFIRES WITH OTHER ROUNDELS

During the war, apart from Great Britain, only three other fighting nations would use the Spitfire versions covered in this publication: Australia, as we have just seen, the United States and the Soviet Union. The Soviets were globally disappointed by the Spitfire Mk.V which they had used as a tactical fighter over the battlefields. However, as their industrial output should have concentrated more on frontline combat aircraft, the USSR soon found itself in need of an interceptor within its air defence units which were stationed, by definition, far from the combat zones. Thus, the Soviets were more than happy to accept the British offer to provide the Spitfire Mk.IX as part of the Lend Lease

Above.
Like many other European countries, Belgium used a great number of Spitfires after the war. The Griffon-engined examples were reserved for the combat units, but the Merlin-engined Mk.IX Spitfires were used for training at the advanced pilot school in Brustem, seen here at the end of the 1940s.
(André Bar)

Below.
The Americans were among the first to take the Spitfire Mk.IX on charge, as early as the Tunisian campaign. Of course, at that time, in early 1943, this relatively rare model was shared between commanding officers, as seen here with Colonel Fred M. Dean, the commander of the 31st FG. It is worth noting that he followed the tradition of using his initials as a tactical code, which is a tradition he borrowed from the RAF wing commanders.

agreement, taking on charge 1,185 planes from February 1944 onwards.

In 1945, 26 of the 81 Soviet air defence regiments used the Spitfire Mk.IX and almost 850 of these planes were still in service when the war came to an end in Europe. The Spitfire was still used beyond the beginning of the Cold War and the last regiments only swapped their Spitfires for more modern planes in 1948.

Given the restricted uses of the Spitfire Mk.VI and Mk.VII, they were not offered for export. At the end of the war they were soon declared obsolete, if this was not already the case. The same applied to the Mk.VIII as it was withdrawn from RAF service and

Above.
Only about 20 Spitfires were converted into two-seaters and few countries were keen on buying them. Egypt bought one sole example, which bore the code 684 and was delivered in 1950.

Below.
French-flown Spitfires from GC II/6 « Nice » taxi into position for their mission into Germany from this snow-covered field in the Vosges foothills, France. A crew chief seated on the wing directs the pilot onto the runway. *(US NARA)*

was thus not widely exported. As we have seen, only Australia used a large number of Mk.VIII during the war. But at the end of the war, the RAAF decided not to retain the Spitfire in its inventory, preferring instead another legendary plane, the P-51 Mustang.

Only fifteen Mk.VIII would bear other roundels, these being those of the Royal Indian Air Force (RIAF) when India gained its independence in 1947. These planes served for a while as fighter trainers, but were soon replaced by more modern aircraft. Nevertheless, they were joined by ten twin-seater Spitfires that were delivered in 1948. India thus became, as far as we know, the biggest user of the twin-seater Spitfire, as we do not know the exact number of planes of this type that were transformed by the Soviets.

As for the Mk.XVI, it was handicapped by the fact that its engine was American-made and supplied as part of the Lend Lease agreement, meaning that the United States had the rights as to how these planes were used. The British had other priorities at the end of the war and tried to avoid paying for these engines initially. Therefore, the exportation of the Mk.XVI was limited to 76 planes supplied to Greece in 1949 when the country was in the throes of a civil war, with these planes being added to the pre-

viously received Mk.IX. The Americans supported the Hellenic monarchy in its fight against communist rebels, bringing in all sorts of military assistance. As Greece already used the Spitfire Mk.V and Mk.IX, the United States accepted the delivery of the Mk.XVI which were also well-suited to the role of ground support. Once the communist threat was removed, the Spitfire was soon replaced by jet aircraft and was definitively withdrawn in 1954.

Great Britain therefore had no other choice than to offer the Spitfire Mk.IX for export in order to bring in sorely needed money. In 1945, this version still had useful capabilities and constituted an interesting low cost alternative for many air forces that were trying to reform or modernise at a time where defence budgets were reduced due to the end of the war. It also meant that they could be used whilst awaiting the finance for the acquisition of the plane of the future, the jet! The first countries to come forward were those who had pilots trained to fly the Spitfire, or those who had flown with them during the war.

Belgium purchased 28 Spitfire Mk.IX at the end of the war to be used as advanced fighter training planes, having chosen the Griffon-engined Spitfire XIV to equip its frontline units. Added to these 28 Mk.IX in 1952 were 15 Mk.IX purchased from Holland, with this version being definitively struck of charge from the Belgian air force inventory two years later.

The two Norwegian RAF squadrons returned to their country in 1945 with 36 brand-new Spitfire Mk.IX, to which were later added another 32. These planes would fly until 1952.

Of the four main dominions, South Africa was the only one to retain the Spitfire in its post-war units. In all, 126 planes made their way to this country between 1947 and October 1949, serving both as frontline or reserve units, as well as flying schools. They were only retired from service in 1954.

Below.
Many Spitfire Mk.XVI units, including the two Belgian units (No 349 and No 350 Squadrons) took part in the occupation of Germany. No 349 Sqn. was led by Raymond "Cheval" Lallemant, the Belgian ace, who joined the ranks of the RAF as early as July 1940. He is seen here in his Spitfire serial TB900 nicknamed "Winston Churchill". Lallemant spent a great part of the war with No 609 Sqn., which was equipped with Typhoons. He was severely wounded in September 1944, but took command of No 349 Sqn. in March 1945, despite not having fully recovered. He remained in the Force Aérienne Belge after the war, becoming a colonel and retiring in 1952. (André Bar)

Burma was a late Spitfire user, taking thirty on charge in 1954, planes they purchased from Israel and which were mainly used for advanced fighter training, even though they were occasionally used against guerilla movements which shook the country during the nineteen-fifties. They were withdrawn from service a few years later.

The Czechoslovakians left for their country in August 1945 with 71 Mk.IX ceded by Great Britain. They were followed by six other planes in 1946-47. Named S-89 in the nomenclature of the new Czechoslovakian air force, they served until 1948 when, due to a regime change, the Spitfire was withdrawn from frontline unit service and replaced by Soviet-made aircraft. Although some were still flying in the following years, 59 of the 62 planes still owned by the Czechoslovakians were sold in 1948-49 to Israel, a country looking for combat aircraft at that time. Denmark reformed its air force from scratch in 1945. As it did not have the means to equip itself with modern aircraft, it chose the Spitfire Mk.IX, taking on charge 38 starting in 1947 (not counting the planes delivered for ground crew training and those used for spare parts). These planes were withdrawn from service in 1955 after having accumulated almost 10,000 flying hours.

The Republic of Ireland also wanted to purchase a few Spitfires, but surprisingly, they only acquired six twin-seater Mk.IX along with a batch of Seafires. These aircraft remained in service until the beginning of the nineteen-sixties.

Italy extensively used the Spitfire Mk.IX with 141 planes taken on charge between 1946 and 1947, to which were added two from Turkey in 1949 (a total of 143 Mk.IX). They equipped two fighter wings (5° and 51° Stormi) and were retired from frontline service in 1950. A few remained in service until 1952 and thirty were sold to Israel.

Turkey also extensively used the Mk.IX. As the Mk.V was already in service in its air force, 170 Mk.IX would arrive in the country between 1947 and 1949. Five regiments flew with the Spitfire, an aircraft that was progressively replaced starting in 1948 within frontline units.

The last of them were finally withdrawn from service in 1954. Although the bulk of post-war purchased Spitfire Mk.IX had peaceful careers, the same could not be said for others. A few exported Spitfire Mk.IX took part in various conflicts, the biggest probably being the Israel – Arab conflict where the two main belligerents (Israel and Egypt) fielded Spitfires. At the end of the Second World War, Egypt already had Mk.V Spitfires, but wishing to upgrade its fleet, it purchased 39 Mk.IX and a twin-seater T.IX in 1946-47. They equipped at this time two fighter units Nos 1 and 2 Squadrons of the Royal Egyptian Air Force (REAF). They played an active role in the Israeli-Arab conflict of 1948, losing several in combat, with at least one being shot down by an Israeli Spitfire. After 1948, the surviving planes were grouped together within No 1 Sqn, and the Spitfire Mk.IX were struck off charge from the beginning of the nineteen-fifties and replaced by more modern aircraft.

Below.
Spitfire Mk.IXc flown by Lt Col E. P. Allen of the XIXth Tactical Air Command at St-Dizier (France) in October 1944. This aircraft has an overall natural metal finish, the rudder only remaining in original camouflage finish. It was rumoured that Allen "traded" a P-47 for this aircraft. *(SDASM)*

Above.
The Heyl Ha 'Avir, the Israeli air force received less than 100 Spitfire Mk.IXs which participated in the fights against Egypt and were removed from the service only in 1956.

Israel acquired its Spitfires in a bit of a hurry, just after the end of the British mandate in Palestine. These planes in fact came from Czechoslovakia which, following a regime change in 1948, was trying to sell its Spitfires. A first batch of 50 planes was acquired in October 1948 and this order soon increased to 59 plus another two for spare parts. To this were added planes captured from Egypt and thirty others purchased from Italy in 1951-52, making approximately 90 planes equipping two fighter units and one for operational transformation. The Israeli Spitfires were of course used in combat and would go on to have a long career as they were used until 1956. As we have already seen, some were then sold to Burma.

France acquired more than 350 Spitfire Mk.IX for its air force and these planes formed the main French post war fighter force, along (with the P-47 Thunderbolt). The Spitfire was the first combat plane that France sent to Indochina when the troubles began in 1947, but their number would always remain below what was really needed and their efficiency there was relative. The Spitfire was replaced by more modern aircraft, as well as ones more suited to this theatre of operations, but all the same, this did not herald the end of the Spitfire's career within the French air force as the latter would use it up to 1953.

The Czechoslovaks did not take part in the occupation of Germany after the war, and returned to their home country with new planes given to them by Great Britain. These pilots subsequently formed the structure of the new post-war Czechoslovak Air Force until the Communists took power in 1948. The Spitfires were subsequently replaced with Soviet-issue equipment and were sold mostly to Israel. Seen here are planes of the 2. Letecka Divize which used the codes and insignia of RAF No 312 Sqn. *(Jiri Rajlich)*

Above. Spitfire LF.IX from the Elliniki Vassiliki Aeroporia (Royal Hellenic Air Force). In 1947, Greece purchased 110 Spitfire LF and HF.IXs for its newly reformed air force and a further 66 Mk.XVIs followed in 1949. (EPA)

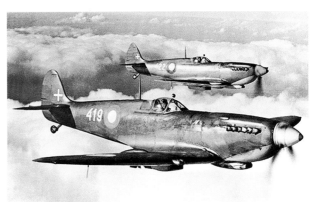

Above. A pair of Royal Danish Air Force Spitfires HF Mk.IX belonging to 5. Eskadrille photographed at altitude, 1949. The aircraft nearer to the camera (No 419/ serial RK811) was an ex-RAF, delivered to Denmark in September 1948. *(Danmarks Flymuseum)*

The French fleet air arm also took on charge twenty Spitfire Mk.IX in 1946 as transitional aircraft for pilots who would go on to fly the Seafires that the French navy had purchased after the war.

Greece also used in combat its 109 Mk.IX taken on charge in 1947 and 1948, planes which replaced the aging Mk.V, used intensively against the communist forces. They were withdrawn from service in 1953.

The Dutch were, like the French, faced with insurrection in their colonies, these being the Dutch Indies. Twenty Mk.IX were purchased and delivered to No 322 Sqn based in this colony and which would carry out missions against the rebels starting in 1947. After the independence of Indonesia, the surviving Spitfires were taken back to

Holland with fifteen being sold to Belgium and three being retired to be used for spare parts. Indeed, Holland no longer needed these Spitfires, which were added to the 38 planes (35 single and three twin-seater) of this version taken on charge in 1946 for use at home as advanced fighter trainers.

The Spitfire was used up to the arrival of the Gloster Meteor in 1951, but its service life was prolonged with the reformation of No 322 Sqn when it returned from the Dutch Indies and which would use this version until autumn 1953.

Other Spitfires also bore other nationality roundels, but this was in fact limited a few planes that were only marginally used.

The Norwegians of No 331 and 332 Squadrons returned to Norway as early as May 1945, but remained under RAF authority until November of the same year. In the meantime, the Norwegian Spitfires were repainted with their nationality markings, as seen here with the rudder painted in the pre-war colours of Norway.

Mark IX

Supermarine Spitfire Mk.IX 5583. Air Operations School of the SAAF. Langebaanweg (South Africa), 1953.
Having used the Spitfire in combat during World War II, the SAAF logically bought Spitfire Mk.IXs once the conflict was over. South Africa was actually the only dominion to do so, as the others (Australia, Canada, New Zealand) preferred American equipment. In total, 136 Spitfires entered the SAAF (serial numbers 5502 to 5637) from 1947 to 1949. After being replaced by jets in the early 1950s, they were used for a few more years in training units.

Mark XVI

Supermarine Spitfire LF.16E TE452. No 5 Squadron. Chivenor (United Kingdom), 1950.
After having fought in the Far East during the war, No 5 Sqn. was reformed in 1949 with the Spitfire LF.16E while it was waiting for its conversion to Meteors in August of the following year. The TE452 seen here was lost in an accident that killed the pilot on 1 August 1950, shortly before the unit stopped using Spitfires.

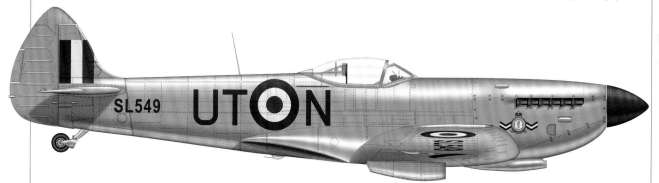

Supermarine Spitfire LF.16E SL549. No 17 Squadron. Chivenor (United Kingdom), 1950.
In February 1949, No 691 Sqn., a unit in cooperation with the Army set up for the training of anti-aircraft personnel, was renamed No 17 Sqn. (its role remained the same nonetheless). Spitfire 16 was just a small part of the squadron's flight equipment, which also comprised of Oxford, Harvard and Beaufighter aircraft. No 517 Sqn. was disbanded in April 1951.

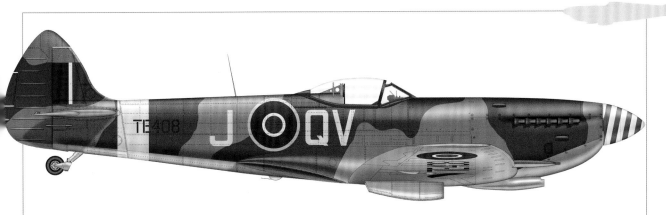

Supermarine Spitfire LF.16E TE408. No 19 Squadron. Wittering (United Kingdom), 1946.
No 19 Sqn., the first unit to use Spitfires, ended the war with Mustangs. Meanwhile, in March 1946, it was temporarily converted to the Spitfire Mk.16 before being equipped with the DH Hornet in October. The propeller cone was painted in blue and white, the colours of the squadron, a distinctive marking that not all Spitfire 16s received given the short period in which they were used.

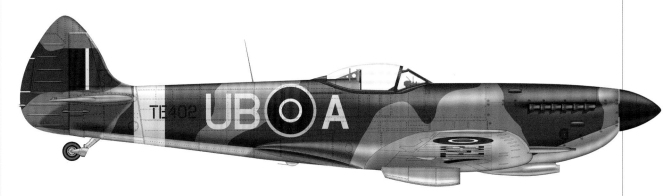

Supermarine Spitfire LF.16E TE402. No 63 Squadron. Middle Wallop (United Kingdom), 1946.
No 63 Sqn. participated in the war in a variety of roles, but was used as fighter unit. During the D-Day landings, its Mk.Vs were notably used for the naval gun spotting. In 1946, No 63 Sqn. became a fighter unit and took the Spitfire Mark 16 on charge, which it used until May 1948, when it was re-equipped with Meteors.

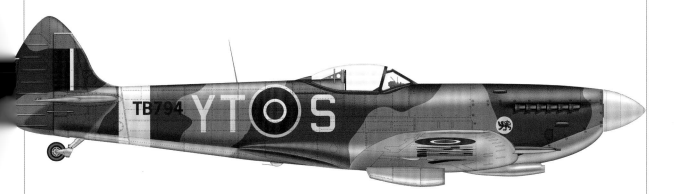

Supermarine Spitfire LF.16E TB794. No 65 Squadron. Hethel (United Kingdom), 1946.
No 65 Squadron found itself in the same situation as No 19 Sqn. when it was decided to take the Mustang out of service. The Spitfire LF.16 was a temporary replacement before the delivery of the D.H. Hornet in the summer of 1946.

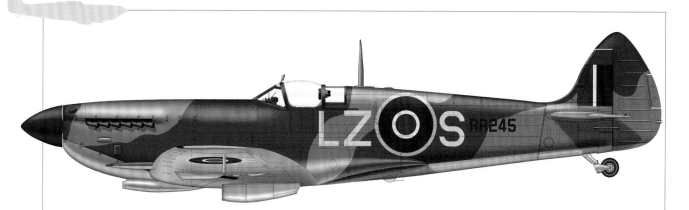

Supermarine Spitfire Mk.XVI RR245. No 66 Squadron. B-60/Grimbergen (Belgium), late 1944.
No 66 Sqn. had fought with Spitfires right from the start of the war and thus used all the major models of the fighter planes flown in Great Britain and in Europe. In November, it switched from the Mk.IX to the Mk.XVI and was appointed to ground attack missions until it was disbanded in April 1945. It only claimed one victory with this version.

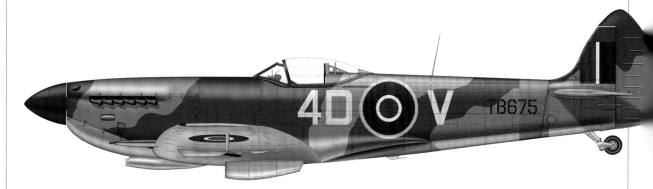

Supermarine Spitfire Mk.XVI TB675. No 74 (Trinidad) Squadron. B-105/Drope (Germany), April 1945.
No 74 Sqn. was the last of four RAF units to be converted to the Mk.XVI, as the transfer took place as late as March 1945. The first sorties were flown on the 9th of the same month. Despite this, more than 800 sorties were flown up to the end of the war.

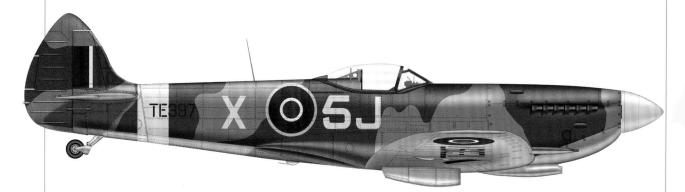

Supermarine Spitfire LF.16E TE397. No 126 (Persian Gulf) Squadron. Hethel (United Kingdom), 1946.
No 126 Sqn. was using Mustangs at the end of the war. When these planes were taken out of service in 1946, the squadron received the Spitfire Mk.XVI as a replacement in February. They were barely used as the squadron was disbanded the following month.

Supermarine Spitfire Mk.XVI RR257. No 127 Squadron. B-60/Grimbergen (Belgium), November 1944.
No 127 Sqn. was the first RAF unit to swap its Mk.IX for Mk.XVIs in November 1944. At that time, invasion stripes were still present on the lower surfaces. This squadron was disbanded on 30 April 1945, after having flown approximately 1,500 sorties with the Mk.XVI.

Supermarine Spitfire Mk.XVI TE206. No 302 (Polish) Squadron. B-113/Varrelbusch (Germany), September 1945.
No 302 Sqn. was one of the two Polish units to transform to the Mk.XVI during the war, thus replacing its Mk.IXs in January 1945. The planes flew 1,300 sorties up to May. No 302 Sqn. afterwards took part in the occupation of Germany and changed its code on this occasion ("QH" replaced "WX").

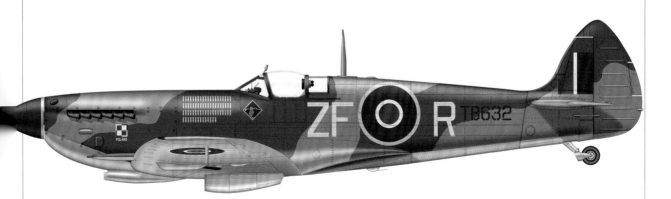

Supermarine Spitfire Mk.XVI TB632. No 308 (Polish) Squadron. B-113/Varrelbusch (Germany), summer 1945.
No 308 (Polish) Squadron's transformation to Mk.XVIs took place at a late stage in March 1945 after having used the Mk.IX for eighteen months. The plane seen here bore an impressive number of mission markings on its engine cowling. The squadron, just like No 302, took part in the occupation of Germany before being disbanded in December 1946.

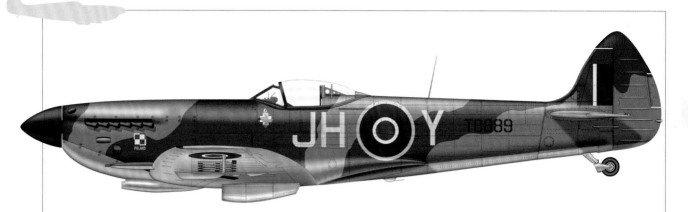

Supermarine Spitfire Mk.XVI TB889. No 317 (Polish) Squadron. B- /Ahlorn (Germany), 1946.
No 317 (Polish) Sqn. fought with the Mk.IX until the end of the war and flew its last sorties on May the 4th. In the same month, as it was sent to Germany, it switched to the Mk.XVI in order to be equipped with the same version as No 302 and 308 Sqns. The squadron was disbanded in December 1946.

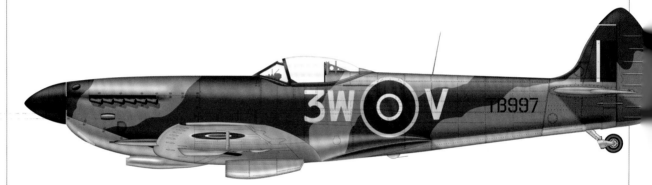

Supermarine Spitfire Mk.XVI TB997. No 322 (Dutch) Squadron. B-106/Twente (Netherlands), April 1945.
Right from its formation, No 322 Sqn. flew Spitfires. It specialised in the hunting down V1 flying bombs. In January 1945, the squadron was based in the Netherlands with its Mk.XVIs. It took part in ground-attack missions against the Germans and flew more than 1,200 sorties in the last four months of the war. TB997 seen here, which was taken on charge in April, does not have the orange triangle, a distinctive marking for planes flown by Dutchmen, but does not appear to have been systematically applied to the Mk.XVI.

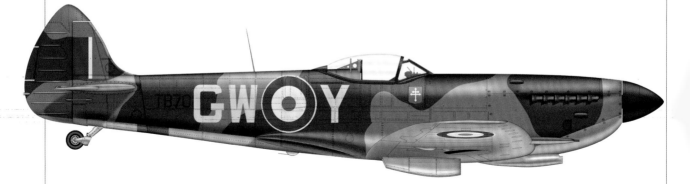

Supermarine Spitfire Mk.XVI TB702. No 340 (French) Squadron. B-105/Drope (Germany), June 1945.
No 340 Sqn. (GC IV/2 "Ile de France"), the first Free French fighter unit, fought the entire war with Spitfires. In February 1945, it transformed from the Mk.IX to the Mk.XVI in order to participate in ground attack missions, of which it flew more than 1,000. No 340 Sqn. kept the Mk.XVI until its transfer to the Armée de l'Air in November 1945.

Supermarine Spitfire Mk.XVI TD388. No 345 (French) Squadron, B.105 Drope (Germany), June 1945.
Three French fighter units serving within the RAF were equipped with the Mk.XVI, the last one being No 345 Sqn. (GC II/2 "Berry") in April 1945. This squadron followed No 340 Sqn. and kept the Mk.XVI until November 1945. From October 1944 onwards, the French units of the RAF were allowed to bear the French roundels, the Croix de Lorraine having been one of their distinctive markings right from the beginning.

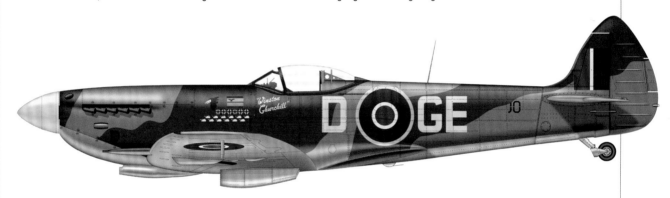

Supermarine Spitfire Mk.XVI TB900. S/L Raymond A. Lallemand (Belgium). No 349 (Belgium) Squadron. B-116/Wunstorf (Germany), June 1945.
During its stay in Great Britain, No 349 Sqn. was used for ground-attack missions, first with the Mk.IX, and then, in the last days of the war, with the Mk.XVI, its last operational sorties taking place on 3 and 4 May. This squadron was placed under the command of Robert "Cheval" Lallemant, a Belgian ace, in March 1945. The plane seen here was taken on charge by the squadron in late April 1945; here, it is seen here with the mid-summer 1945 livery.

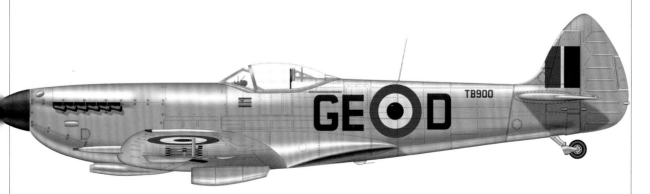

Supermarine Spitfire LF.16 TB900. S/L Albert van der Velde. No 349 (Belgium) Squadron. B-152 /Fassberg (Germany), 1946.
When Albert van der Velde replaced Lallemant in December 1945, he logically inherited TB900 as his personal plane, which was, at the time, entirely in bare metal with Belgian roundels. The "GE" code was moved to the other side of the roundel.

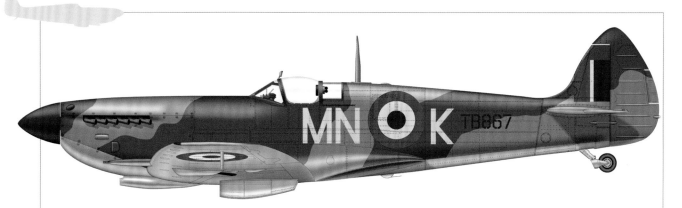

Supermarine Spitfire LF.16 TB867. No 350 (Belgium) Squadron. B-152/Fassberg (Germany), 1946.
No 350 Sqn., which took part in the occupation of Germany, transformed to the Mk.XVI in January 1946 in order to have
the same equipment as No 349 Sqn. TB867 seen here was afterwards loaned to the *Force Aérienne Belge* while they
waited for delivery of the Mk.XIV's and was withdrawn from service in August 1947.

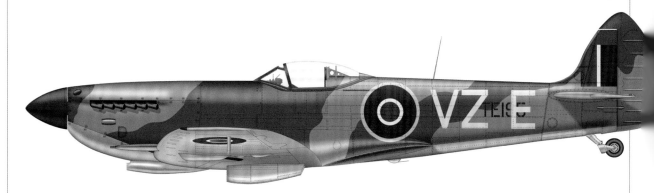

Supermarine Spitfire Mk.XVI TE195. No 412 (RCAF) Squadron. B-152/Fassberg (Germany), summer 1945.
No 412 RCAF Sqn. fought with the Mk.IX until the German capitulation. When it was posted to the Germany occupation forces, it switched
to the Mk.XVI as early as May 1945, but shortly afterwards received the Griffon-engined Mk.XIV in June.

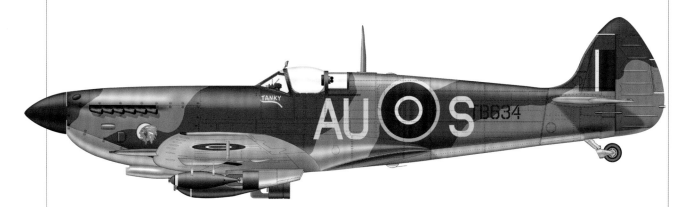

Supermarine Spitfire Mk.XVI TB634. No 421 (RCAF) Squadron. B-90/Kleine Brogel (Germany), March 1945.
No 421 RCAF Sqn., part of the 2 TAF, was equipped with Mk.XVIs in December 1944 and flew more than 2,000 sorties with this model up to
May 1945. It received the Griffon-engined Mk.XIV in September while it was stationed in Germany.

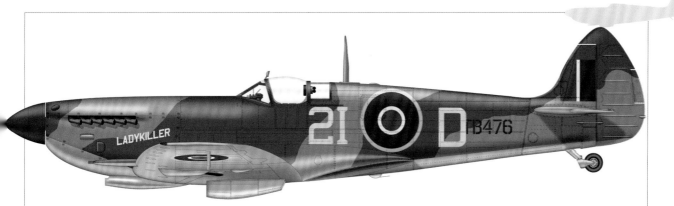

Supermarine Spitfire LF.XVI TB476, S/L Arthur H. "Art" Sager, No 443 (RCAF) Squadron. B-90/Kleine Brogel (Belgium), March 1945.
As part of the 2 TAF, No 443 Canadian Sqn. was the last of the four Canadian units to be operational with this version. Despite their ground-attack role, the squadron claimed two victories in the last days of the war. In the first weeks of using this version, the unit was led by Art Sager, an ace, who was on his second tour of operations that ended in March 1945.

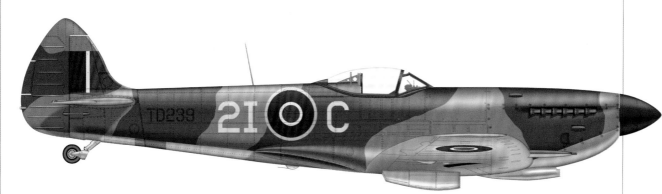

Supermarine Spitfire LF.XVIE TD239, S/L Thomas J. De Courcy, No 443 (RCAF) Squadron B.154/Reinsehlen (Germany), June 1945.
Art Sager was replaced by S/L de Courcy in the last days of the war; as a personal plane, he used one of the first Spitfires with a tear-drop cockpit taken on charge by No 443 Sqn. It was whilst flying this plane, and with the help of two other pilots, that he shot down a Ju 88 on 3 May 1945, which was to be the squadron's last victory. De Courcy died in a car accident one month later.

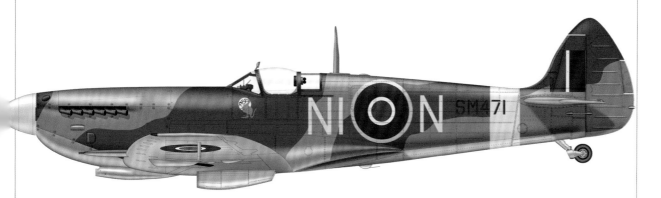

Supermarine Spitfire LF.XVIE SM471. No 451 (RCAF) Squadron. Swanington (United Kingdom), March 1945.
After having fought in the Mediterranean for three years, RCAF No 451 Sqn. was sent to Great Britain, where its main mission was to attack V1 sites with their Mk.XVIs, as well as escorting Bomber Command aircraft which had began flying daylight raids again in spring 1945. Meanwhile, the squadron's activity was reduced, with less than 400 sorties on the Mk.XVI.

Supermarine Spitfire LF.XVIE SM256. No 453 (RAAF) Squadron. Swanington (United Kingdom), late 1944.
For a long time, No 453 Sqn. was the only Australian fighter unit to be based in Great Britain, until it was rejoined by No 451 Sqn. It had been using the Mk.XVI since November 1944, with which it attacked V2 launch sites on the continent under the leadership of Fighter Command, totalising more than 1,000 sorties with this version up to the end of the war. The difference concerning the camouflage scheme on the upper engine cowling is due to the fact that this part has been taken off another plane.

Supermarine Spitfire LF.XVIE TB675. No 485 (NZ) Squadron. Fassberg (Germany), summer 1945.
No 485 (New Zealand) Sqn. ended the war with the Mk.IX. But as it was afterwards attached to a Mk.XVI-equipped wing as part of the occupation of Germany, the squadron switched to the Mk.XVI in May 1945, with a large number of planes coming from No 74 Sqn. which had returned to Great Britain. TB675 seen here was one of the planes that retained their individual letters (see also No 74 Sqn.'s TB675). No 485 Sqn. was disbanded in August 1945.

Supermarine Spitfire LF.16E SL669. No 501 (County of Gloucester) Squadron. Middle Wallop (United Kingdom), 1947.
After having ended the war with Hawker Tempests, No 501 Sqn. was disbanded before being re-formed in May 1946. It was attached to the Auxiliary Air Force. It received the Spitfire Mk.16 which it used until 1949, when it transformed to Vampires.

Supermarine Spitfire LF.16E TE437. No 603 (City of Edinburgh) Squadron. Turnhouse (United Kingdom), 1947.
No 603 Sqn. ended the war with the Spitfire Mk.XVI; it was disbanded on 15 August 1945, but was recreated in May of the following year and attached to the Auxiliary Air Force where it received the Mk.16, which it kept until June 1948, when it transferred to the Mk.22. The RAuxAF units were identified by the three-letter squadron code.

Supermarine Spitfire LF.16E TB911. No 609 (West Riding) Squadron. Yeadon (United Kingdom), 1950.
Typhoon-equipped No 609 was disbanded in September 1945. In 1947, it was first recreated as a night-fighter unit equipped with the Mosquito NF.30, and then, in April 1948, became a day-fighter unit with the RAuxAF and was issued with the Spitfire Mk.16. They were replaced by the Vampire FB.5 in 1950.

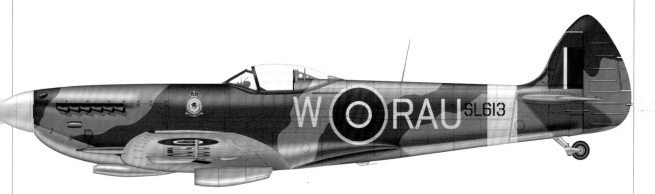

Supermarine Spitfire LF.16E SL613. No 614 (County of Glamorgan) Squadron. Llandwon (United Kingdom), 1947.
No 614 Sqn. was re-formed in May 1946 as part of the Auxiliary Air Force. It was equipped with the Spitfire Mk.16 for two and a half years, and then transformed to the Spitfire F.22. It was also the only Welsh unit within the RAuxAF.

Supermarine Spitfire LF.16E SL614. No 631 Squadron. Llanbedr (United Kingdom), 1946.
The Spitfire Mk.16 not only served among regular or reserve units, as it was also used by second line units such No 631 Sqn., which was tasked with operating with the Army. No 631 was created in 1943 and flew different types of planes, including Spitfires. The Mk.16 was delivered in June 1945 and was used until 1949, when the unit was renamed No 20 Sqn. The propeller cone and the individual letter were painted yellow, in order to make them more visible on the ground. Logically, this Spitfire was not armed.

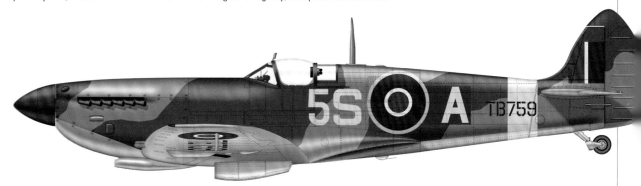

Supermarine Spitfire LF.16E TB759. No 691 Squadron. Chivenor (United Kingdom), 1948.
No 691 had a career similar to that of No 631 as it was given the same missions. The squadron used the Spitfire Mk.16 from August 1945 to February 1949, when it was renamed No 17 Sqn.

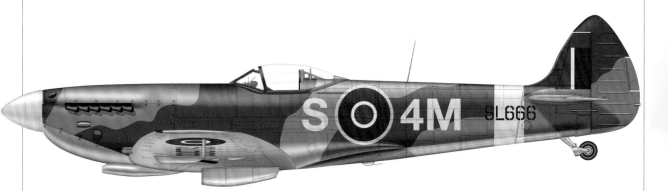

Supermarine Spitfire LF.16E SL666. No 695 Squadron. North Weald (United Kingdom), 1946.
No 695 Sqn. was created in December 1943 in order to train ground troops in anti-aircraft shooting. In July 1945, the squadron received the Spitfire Mk.XVI, which was then flying side by side with the Oxford, Harvard and other types of planes. No 695 was renamed No 34 Sqn. in 1949.

Supermarine Spitfire LF.16E TE389. No 236 OCU. Kinloss (United Kingdom), 1949.
At the end of the war, the RAF underwent a restructuring; Operational Conversion Units (OCU) were created in order to take the role of many advanced training units. No 236 OCU was under Coastal Command control and had, among others, two Spitfire Mk.16s along with 20 Lancaster GR.IIIs and five Beaufighter TF.X. The code is reversed here, as the one normally attributed to No 236 OCU was "K7".

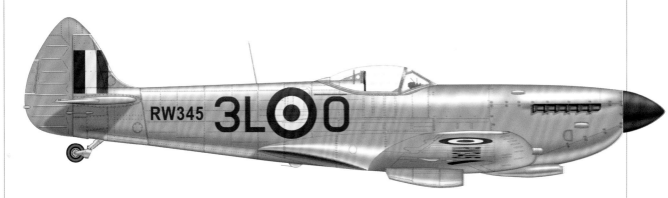

Supermarine Spitfire LF.16 RW345. FCCRS (Fighter Command Control & Reporting School). Middle Wallop (United Kingdom), late 1940s.
Among the second line units using the Spitfire Mk.16 after the war was the Fighter Command Control and Reporting School, a small unit in charge of air detection.

Supermarine Spitfire LF.16 TE203. No 1 (P)RFU. Finingley (United Kingdom), late 1940s.
The Spitfire 16 saw great use by training units, such as No 1 (Pilot) Refresher Flying Unit, which was in charge of refresher courses for pilots who had served too long in headquarters. This type of unit used a variety of planes. The code of this unit was made up of three letters, the last one being the individual letter (seen here is the letter A).

91

Supermarine Spitfire LF.16 RW396. Central Gunnery School. Leconfield (United Kingdom), late 1940s.
The Central Gunnery School was also a training unit that used the Mk.16. Its code was made up of three letters (FJW). The unit was in charge of improving the pilots' in-flight firing. RW396 seen here was destroyed in an accident in January 1949.

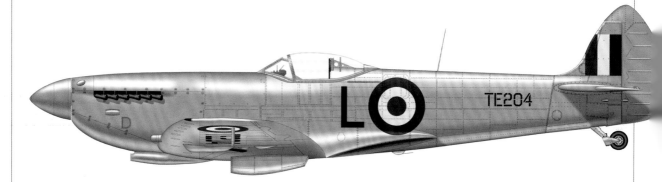

Supermarine Spitfire LF.16 TE204. No 3 Civilian Anti-Aircraft Cooperation Unit. Exeter (United Kingdom), early 1950s.
No 3 Civilian Anti-Aircraft Cooperation Unit, created in March 1951 in order to take on the tasks that had belonged up to then to No 17 Sqn., possessed a great diversity of planes, including some Spitfire Mk.16s. The markings on these planes were very low-key, with only one letter painted in front of the roundel. The TE204 was taken out of service in December 1954 and was one of the last Spitfire Mk.16 still in service in the RAF. It was put in storage for a year and a half before being scrapped.

Supermarine Spitfire LF.XVIE TB520. Wing Commander Donald G. Andrews (RAAF). Matlask (United Kingdom), March 1945.
Don Andrews was an Australian pilot who served in Great Britain from late 1941 onwards. In 1942, he found himself in No 453 (Australian) Squadron, where he took the command of a flight before becoming squadron leader. For his final tour of operations in 1945, Andrews took over the Coltishall wing (which included No 451 and 453 (Australian) Squadrons, equipped with the Mk.XVI), and, given that the RAF allowed it, painted his initials on the plane as his code. He also retained his personal insignia that he had used since his posting to No 453 Sqn. However, the Australian flag on the tail fin was a tolerated rule infringement that appeared on only a few Spitfires (especially among No 453 Sqn.) in the last weeks of the war.

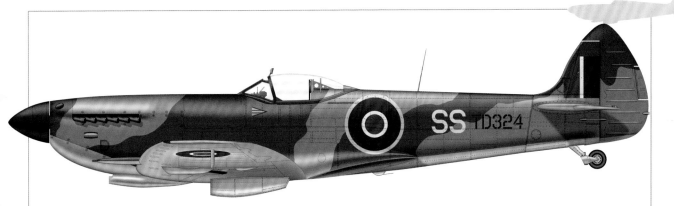

Supermarine Spitfire LF.XVIE TD324. Wing Commander Ralph W. F. Sampson. B-105/Drope (Germany), summer 1945.
"Sammy" Sampson was an ace who served, among others, in Nos 602, 131 and 127 Sqns., the latter being on the Mk.XVI, before becoming WingCo flyingof No 145 Wing in 1945, a wing which included a certain number of French units also using the Mk.XVI. He stepped down from his post as commander in August 1945, his personal plane at the time being TD324 seen here.

Supermarine Spitfire LF.XVIE TB300. Group Captain Percival S. Turner. No 127 Wing, Germany, early 1945.
"Stan" Turner was a Canadian of English descent who enlisted in the RAF before the war. Given his career at the time, he was naturally given a place within No 242 (Canadian) Sqn. with which he served with distinction during the Battles of France and Britain. In 1945, he was named leader of No 127 Wing, which was mostly made up of RCAF squadrons. He finished the war with 11 confirmed victories to his name, one of which in was shared. He continued his career with the RCAF after the war. Like all wing commanders, he had the initials of his surname and first name on his aircraft. Whereas the insignia on the nose of the plane was that of No 421 (Canadian) Sqn., the plane being probably maintained by this unit.

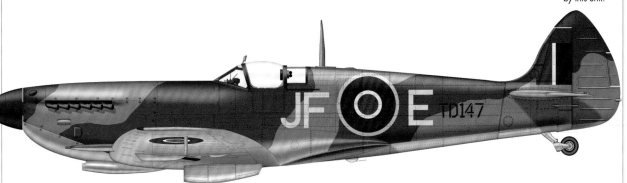

Supermarine Spitfire LF.XVIE TD147. Wing Commander James F. Edwards (RCAF). No 127 Wing. Germany, spring 1945.
Even though G/C Turner was at the head of No 127 Wing, leadership for operational missions was handed over, in April 1945, to "Eddie" Edwards, a Canadian with 18 kills (3 of which were shared), and who established his reputation in the desert flying Kittyhawks. Edwards claimed his final two kills whilst flying TD147 seen here: two damaged planes on 29 April and the shooting down a Ju 88 (shared) on 3 May. Edwards continued his career with the RCAF after the war.

CAMOUFLAGE SCHEMES AND MARKINGS

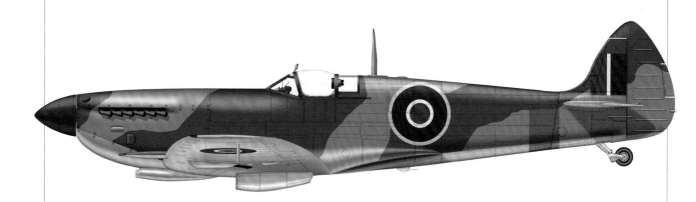

In Europe

The Spitfire MK.IX entered into service at a time when camouflage schemes and markings had stabilised. Since 15 August 1941, the planes had been painted in Ocean Grey and Dark Green for the upper surfaces, and Medium Sea Grey for the lower surfaces, these being the new standard colour tones for the RAF in Europe. Indeed, since the beginning of 1941, Fighter Command had gone onto the offensive over the Continent and its aircraft, therefore, regularly found themselves over the Channel or northern Europe where the countryside was not always the same as in Great Britain. As Dark Earth had been deemed too visible, it was replaced by a more neutral colour which could be used both over water and the ground of northern Europe. Ocean Grey was in fact a good compromise, whilst Medium Sea Grey was also deemed more suitable than Sky which sometimes stood out too much against the north European sky. These colours thus became standard for the new Day Fighter Scheme.

In order to be more recognisable during frontal phases of a dogfight where it was easy to mix up outlines of various aircraft, a four-inch stripe was painted on the leading edge of the wings. The propellor cone, 18-inch fuselage stripe and code letters remained in Sky. These markings were, however, only applied to Fighter Command aircraft—followed by the ADGB—, and were not present on Spitfires in service outside of the latter two organisations, with the exception of the yellow leading edges which were generalised, but not always systematically, after a period of time in the workshops.

Planes still in production followed these new directives to the letter, in particular the Spitfire Mk.IX, and all bore the new C3 type roundel which was introduced in May 1942. From this date onwards, the Fighter Command/ADGB planes did not undergo any camouflage scheme or marking changes practically up to the end of the war.

This camouflage scheme also became standard for fighters based overseas, starting in 1944 for the Mediterranean, and 1945 for the Far-East, even though they were in the minority in this region when the war ended. The factories often applied markings, with Sky for the propellor cones and yellow for the fuselage band and leading edges; these markings were then repainted, with either red or black for the cone, or by using one of the other two camouflage colours for the other markings. However, by the end of the war, the fuselage band had often been retained, or repainted white in some cases. On the other hand, it would appear that the yellow leading edges were retained.

The Spitfire versions designed for high-altitude flying, such as the Mk.VI or HF.IX, were usually painted according to the Day Fighter Scheme standard, but it was not uncommon to see them painted with colours normally reserved for high-altitude reconnaissance planes, such as the PR.XI, in PR Blue, which appears to have been standard for the Mk.VII. However, as the Mk.VII was more often used for the same missions as the Mk.IX due to a lack of high-altitude targets in 1944, the Mk.VII were progressively repainted in the standard Day Fighter Scheme.

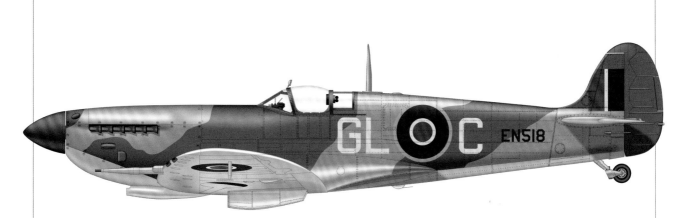

Overseas

The Desert Scheme

This was a scheme that evolved a lot in 1940, the year in which it was introduced, then again in 1942 when the Spitfire first began to be used in the Middle-East. At that time, the scheme had been standardised with Dark Earth and Middle Stone for the upper surfaces, and Sky for the lower surfaces. However, at the same time, Azure Blue was introduced for the lower surfaces, followed in 1943 by Light Mediterranean Blue. The Spitfires

flying in North Africa, the Middle-East, Sicily and the first weeks of the Italian campaign, were painted thus, with mostly Azure Blue in 1942, and Light Mediterranean Blue in 1943. A few planes based in Malta were also painted in this way, especially in 1942, but it would appear that they were repainted as soon as it was possible to do so. The leading edges were usually painted yellow, in the same way as the planes based in Great Britain.

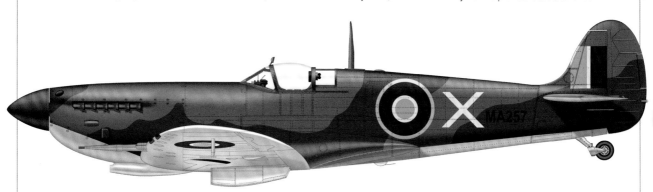

Temperate Land Scheme

This scheme, which was in use before the war, mostly comprised of Dark Earth and Dark Green. It was standard up to 15 August 1941 for RAF fighters in Europe, with the lower surfaces sometimes being in several colours (see previously). In Malta and the Mediterranean in general, it remained in use until 1944, along with Sky, Azure Blue or Light Mediterranean Blue. When the Allies landed in Italy in mid-1943, a lot of Spitfires

painted with the Desert Scheme and which were sent to the rear for an overhaul or major repairs, were repainted with this camouflage scheme, to such an extent that towards the end of 1943, it became the standard scheme. It began to be replaced by the new Day Fighter Scheme from 1944 onwards. However, it remained in use until the end of the war in the Far-East, with Sky for the lower surfaces.

The Spitfire Mk.IX only saw one change to this camouflage scheme in the last three years of the war with the so-called 'invasion' or 'D-Day' stripes painted on all aircraft due to fly over the combat zones. Hastily painted on in the hours before D-Day, these black and white stripes were added to the wings and fuselage. Comprising of three white and two black stripes, they were 18 inches wide (approximately 45 cm) and started 6 inches (roughly 15 cm) from the upper wing roundel, with those of the fuselage starting 18 inches from the tail fin. This meant that the fuselage stripes masked the code letters with a good part of the serial often being hidden too. It was up to the ground crew, therefore, to try their best to leave them visible, either by repainting the letters elsewhere, or by leaving them where they were when the invasion stripes were added.

These stripes would see several changes. Starting on 6 July 1944, they were officially removed from the planes' upper surfaces, wings and fuselage. The fuselage stripes were then moved up covering a third of the fuselage, without there being any real regulations as to how this was carried out, with the squadrons deciding themselves. Between 25 August and 10 September 1944, the stripes still present under the wings were removed, but some planes continued to fly with them until 3 January 1945. They were removed at the same time as the Sky fuselage band whilst the roundels were modified at the same time. Indeed, the Type III roundel was now back in its usual six emplacements. The lower surface roundels received a yellow border, those of

the upper surfaces also had the yellow border, but had an additional white circle between the red and the blue. These markings remained in use until the end of the war.

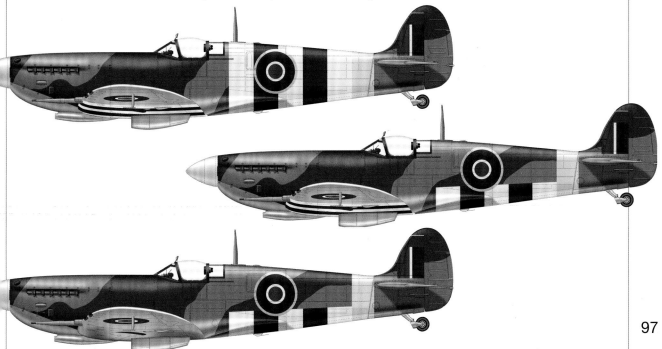

Design and layout Jean-Baptiste Mongin, for Histoire & Collections
Collection manager Dominique Breffort
© Histoire & Collections 2015

ISBN: 978-2-35250-366-8
Publisher's number: 35250
Dépôt légal: 1st quarter 2015

Book edited by
HISTOIRE & COLLECTIONS
SA au capital de 182 938, 82 €
5, avenue de la République
75011 Paris - France
Tel: +33 (0) 1 40 21 18 20
Fax: +33 (0) 1 47 00 51 11
www.histoireetcollections.com

This book has been designed, typed,
laid-out and processed
by Histoire & Collections.

Color separation: Studio H&C
Print by Calidad Grafica,
Spain, European Union,
March 2015.